# THE UNITED STATES IN CRISIS

# THE UNITED STATES IN CRISIS

## Citizenship, Immigration, and the Nation State

EDWARD J. ERLER

CLAREMONT BOOKS

Encounter BOOKS

NEW YORK · LONDON

First American edition published in 2022 by Encounter Books, an activity of Encounter for Culture and Education, Inc., a nonprofit, tax-exempt corporation.
Encounter Books website address: www.encounterbooks.com

Manufactured in the United States and printed on acid-free paper. The paper used in this publication meets the minimum requirements of ANSI/NISO Z39.48–1992 (R 1997) (*Permanence of Paper*).

FIRST EDITION

LIBRARY OF CONGRESS CATALOGING-IN-PUBLICATION DATA

Names: Erler, Edward J., author.
Title: The United States in Crisis: Citizenship, Immigration, and the Nation State / Edward J. Erler.
Description: First American edition. | New York: Encounter Books, 2022. | Includes bibliographical references and index. |
Identifiers: LCCN 2021045806 (print) | LCCN 2021045807 (ebook) | ISBN 9781641772358 (hardcover) | ISBN 9781641772365 (ebook)
Subjects: LCSH: Citizenship—United States. | United States—Emigration and immigration. | Sovereignty. | State, The.
Classification: LCC JK1759 .E75 2022(print) | LCC JK1759 (ebook) | DDC 323.60973—dc23/eng/20211018
LC record available at https://lccn.loc.gov/2021045806
LC ebook record available at https://lccn.loc.gov/2021045807

1 2 3 4 5 6 7 8 9 20 22

*TO MY STUDENTS*

# | CONTENTS |

## CHAPTER ONE

# WHY SOVEREIGNTY MATTERS

ARISTOTLE, IN THE *POLITICS*, noted the tendency of democracies and republics to become oligarchies: the rule of the few for the benefit of the few. On occasion, he noted, one of the oligarchs appeals to the people for their support in overturning the oligarchic class and returning to the old regime.

In his 2016 presidential campaign, then-candidate Trump argued that, while the United States still adhered to republican constitutional forms, the ruling Washington establishment and its allies in finance, big tech and social media had become a thoroughgoing oligarchic combination of ruling elites.

Self-interest is not always the dominant motivating force in some men; sometimes an instinct for justice prevails, or sometimes a reputation for justice might be a primary self-interest. Donald Trump didn't know about Aristotle – or Aristotle's dictum that it is justice, above all, that preserves regimes – but he did understand one thing: it takes an insider to understand oligarchy.

Trump announced that he was a wealthy insider who was outraged at the crimes committed by the oligarchy at the expense of the people – most vividly, how it was profiting from cheap manufacturing China at the expense of the American middle and working classes. This, he believed, was unjust; he wanted to act on behalf of the people to restore the constitutional republic in which the people, rather than the oligarchy, held sovereign power.

In his campaign against the American oligarchy, he appealed

to the closely tied ideas of citizenship, sovereignty, and borders. Bypassing the ruling class elites that dominate the media, the universities, professional political class, and government bureaucrats, Trump's campaign was a direct appeal to the people as the ultimate source of sovereign authority.

In 2016, Trump dominated the media because he was newsworthy. He received free coverage, much of it live, where he could speak directly to the people. He also had free access to millions of Americans on social networks like Twitter and Facebook, allowing him to bypass the corporate media. These networks also allowed Trump's supporters to organize and build alternate communications nodes used to combat media disinformation campaigns.

His stunning victory that November was a defeat for the oligarchy in Washington – including the leadership of both the Democrat and Republican party machines. Both the interests and ideologies of both parties' elites transcended party differences, so they had a large stake in defending their entrenched privileges and their worldviews. Unused to being displaced, this class didn't take defeat lightly. Amplified by their courtiers in corporate media, they formed a chorus that questioned legitimacy of Trump's election even before his Inauguration Day. Talk of his impeachment began almost immediately.

The elites, in and out of government, mobilized against him with resources that he could not match. Throughout his presidency and culminating in the 2020 campaign, the oligarchy would continue its relentless opposition with ever-greater boldness and recklessness. It was able to marshal a near monopoly of the mainstream media, education, entertainment, and business into what amounted to tens of thousands of partisan political operatives, all practicing fanatical message discipline. They spoke with a single voice: the nationalist Donald Trump was synonymous with evil. His domestic policies were "white supremacy" or "fascism"; his foreign policies were "treason."

For many voters of both parties, the hysteria of these elite offensives against Trump revealed the extent to which American democracy had, indeed, transmogrified into an oligarchy, powered by the big tech companies on which modern life depends. That oligarchy was at odds with the nation's traditional conceptions of sovereignty and citizenship. As the 2020 election loomed, the largest Silicon Valley corporations began to realize the massive power they had to shape or disfigure public opinion; it was, after on, on their social media networks that Trump had been able to communicate with his audience and bypass the corporate media.

Using algorithmic manipulation that amounted to censorship, these social networks could deprive Republicans of connecting with their fellow citizens or refuting the dozens of new hoaxes that emanated daily from Trump-hating, partisan journalists. If 2016 had the Steele Dossier and the Russian Collusion narrative – both of which turned out to be hoaxes – then a steady stream of misrepresentations and fabrications became standard fare in 2020. The big tech oligarchs dogged him unmercifully, censoring him at crucial moments that amounted to clear instances of election interference. All of this was in the service of destroying the ideas of citizenship, borders, and nationalism Trump represented and articulated, however imperfectly. He defended American exceptionalism because he understood the importance of sovereignty to national independence and individual liberty.

## A "SEPARATE AND EQUAL" NATION

In becoming "one people," according to the words of the Declaration of Independence, Americans also became a "separate and equal" nation, whose citizens shared equal rights and privileges under the rule of law. These were privileges that remained exclusive to citizenship and were integral to what it meant to be part of a people who shared the same political principles.

More than a century ago, the U.S. Supreme Court announced what was considered to be the settled sense of the matter:

> [I]t is an accepted maxim of international sovereignty, and essential to self-preservation, to forbid the entrance of foreigners within its dominions, or to admit them only in such cases and upon such conditions as it may see fit to prescribe.[1]

A half-century later, the Court reiterated that "the exclusion of aliens is a fundamental act of sovereignty. The right to do so stems not alone from legislative power but is inherent in the executive power to control the foreign affairs of the nation."[2] Thus, according to the Court, regulation of immigration is a matter of both legislative and executive power. The Congress, of course, has been delegated exclusive power in the Constitution "to establish an uniform Rule of Naturalization" which, by necessary inference, includes the power to pass uniform rules governing immigration.* But both decisions refer to the power over immigration that is inherent in executive power: it is essential to national security ("self-preservation") and to foreign policy. This recognition was undoubtedly behind Congress's decision to delegate broad authority over immigration to the executive in the Immigration and Naturalization Act of 1952. Few limits have been placed on the president's broad authority to act under its provisions, which obviously have national security and foreign policy implications.

Progressive constitutional scholars, though, have advanced the theory that there are no enumerated powers in the Constitution to protect the nation's borders. These scholars – who would not ordinarily seek to limit the reach of government by invoking

---

* Professor Ilya Somin, widely known as a libertarian, denies that Congress's enumerated power to establish uniform rules for naturalization implicates any power to legislate on matters of immigration, nor, he argues, can the power to regulate immigration be derived from the "necessary and proper" clause. Libertarianism and progressive liberalism seem to agree on open borders, meaning the nation cannot be sovereign. See Ilya Somin, "Does the Constitution Give the Federal Government Power Over Immigration?" https://www.cato-unbound.org/issues/september-2018/immigration-constitution

enumerated powers – have suddenly hit upon an argument that, if taken seriously, would make it impossible for the United States to maintain itself as a sovereign nation. Protection of citizens by preserving the integrity of the nation's borders is inherent in the idea of sovereignty. Yet, the newfound argument of these Progressive scholars (who have fallen into league with libertarian constitutionalists on the issue of nationalism) has meshed nicely with the most radical elements of the Democratic Party who have proposed abolishing Immigration and Customs Enforcement.

In the postmodern world, the nation-state is under attack everywhere as the source of every imaginable evil. It is said to be the cause of war, selfishness, racism, white privilege, misogyny, homophobia, transphobia, Islamophobia, and all the other so-called irrational phobias that make up the universe of political correctness. It is also said, in the same quarters, that the concept of the nation-state itself is irrational and arbitrary.

It is clear that Progressives no longer views self-preservation as a rational goal of the nation-state; rather, self-preservation must be subordinate to openness and diversity. President Barack Obama gave a notorious answer to a question he was asked at a press conference after a NATO summit meeting in Strasbourg, France, in April 2009. When asked whether he believed in American exceptionalism, as some of his predecessors did, or whether he had a different philosophy, the president gave a curious, but typical Progressive answer: "I believe in American exceptionalism, just as I suspect that the Brits believe in British exceptionalism and the Greeks believe in Greek exceptionalism." But, as the president must have known, if every country is exceptional, then no country is exceptional.

In the universe of cultural relativism that Progressives inhabit, the claim that one nation is exceptional is tantamount to asserting the superiority of that nation and its political principles; this is something intolerable under the canons of cultural relativism that demand that all cultures must be deemed equal. Obama's Secretary of State, John Kerry, spelled out the implications of the president's revealing statement about American exceptionalism when he advised his fellow citizens "to prepare [themselves] for a borderless world."[3]

A "world without borders" will, of course, be a world without sovereign nation-states and, consequently, a world without citizens. The idea of "citizens of the world" is a simple solecism.

All this overwrought criticism of nationalism and the nation-state overlooks a very significant point: the nation-state is the only form of political organization that can sustain constitutional government and the rule of law. If, as is widely alleged, the dialectic of History is inevitably tending toward global governance and universal citizenship – what could be called a "universal homogenous state" – History is also tending toward tyranny. No empire has ever been a constitutional democracy or republic; indeed, constitutional government cannot exist in global government.

A "world without borders" will be a universal and homogeneous state – the European Union on a world scale. But there will be no citizens in this universal state; rather, there will be clients who are ruled by unelected bureaucrats or administrative experts, much like the EU is governed today. These experts rule without the inconvenience of having to consult or rely on the consent of the people because, in this new world, rule by administration – cloaked in what is claimed to be the objective sheen of expertise, or "science" – has replaced politics and political choice. Administrators know what is good for the people better than the people themselves. Freedom to choose has been rendered superfluous.

In fact, freedom has been revealed to be a dangerous delusion, itself dispelled by science. Welfare has replaced freedom as a goal in the universal community, and whatever the administrators decide can be translated directly into practice because the universal homogeneous state will not be a free state. Choice frequently leads to bad decisions; the administrative state will therefore eliminate choice and the possibility of the mistakes that accompany choice. In other words, it will be tyranny.

Tyranny will not be alleviated by the fact that it is based on Progressive science and administered for the good of humanity. This universal tyranny will be no different – no less severe, no less degrading – than tyrannies of the past. In fact, this universal tyranny will bring a new kind of terror and violence to its rule; it will be more efficient and more pervasive because it will be backed by the innovations of science and justified by the advancement of the human estate, the professed goal of modern science from its very beginning. Its protestations of a benign purpose, however, will be a thin disguise for its brutal and psychologically devastating reality.

Citizens (as opposed to clients) can exist only in "separate and equal nations" where exclusive rights and privileges belong to "one people" who have consented to become members of a political community. Free government – constitutional government and the rule of law – has existed only in separate, sovereign nations. The best guarantee of a peaceful and free world is not a global state, but a system of nation-states made up of liberal democracies. Such nations rarely (if ever) go to war with one another.

When President Trump won the presidential election in 2016 with an explicit appeal to restore the American nation-state, the Left redoubled its attacks on the nation-state as a source of a multitude of evils. Nationalism, we were assured, breeds extremism, leads inevitably to wars, racism, ethnic animosities, exclusivity, corporate exploitation and many other intractable political problems. The way to defeat these evils is for nations to band together into international organizations of one sort or another in order to dilute or defeat the ill-effects of nationalism.

## UNIVERSAL VALUES HERE AND ABROAD

Standing before the Arc de Triomphe at an event marking the 100th anniversary of the end of World War I, French President Emmanuel Macron perfectly captured the sentiment of continental and Progressive elites on the issue of nationalism. While never mentioning his American counterpart by name, Macron's remarks were clearly intended to be a stinging rebuke to President Trump, who was present at the speech. The millions who died in the Great War, Macron declared, were fighting to defend the "universal values" (*valeurs universelles*) of France, those values that rejected, "the selfishness of nations only looking after their own interests."

"Patriotism," Macron avowed, "is the exact opposite of nationalism; nationalism is its betrayal" (*trahision*). The patriotic Frenchmen who fought bravely in the First World War would no doubt be surprised by the president's revisionist history. It is difficult to believe that the soldiers who endured such great sacrifices in the defense of France were not inspired and sustained through their long ordeal by a deep sense of patriotism. In fact, it is utterly impossible to believe that such great sacrifices could have been mounted on behalf of abstract "universal values" only remotely connected to their homeland. Does anyone believe these warriors were concerned with eradicating the "egoism" of nations? This surely exceeds the wildest postmodern fantasy that seems to have inspired Macron's attack on the nation-state. The men who fought the Great War were not postmodernists; they fought for their homeland because they were patriots.

For Macron – and the many internationalists and globalists who share his views – nationalism is the very definition of war itself. The egoism and self-aggrandizement they believe is inherent in the idea of nationalism means war is inherent in the very idea of nationalism. This is standard fare in Progressive ideology. It may be impossible to eradicate the egoism of individuals (their desire to rule) but, they believe, the eradication of the nation-state may eliminate or diminish the force of national egoism in the world. International alliances and cooperative organizations can replace the nation-state and eliminate the egoistic and jingoistic conflicts that are inspired by the world of independent, sovereign nations. International and global organizations are the rational answer to the endless conflicts and wars that exist among sovereign nations that have grown not by rational choice, but by accident and force. The universal homogeneous state, we are assured by the globalists, will be the ultimate expression of the rational state.

The rule of law in constitutional democracy means that those who are subject to the law must participate in the making of the law. This is generally done through regularly scheduled elections, where the people elect representatives who make laws designed to secure the "safety and happiness" of the people. Through elections, the people demonstrate their sovereign power and renew their consent to be governed. This represents constitutional democracy's translation of the people's right to revolution into constitutional elections. Elections "constitutionalize" the right of revolution, but the people can never give up or delegate the right of revolution, which is inherent in their sovereignty.[4]

The experts who administer the universal homogeneous state will rule by fiat rather than the rule of law, and their authority will be their scientific expertise. The universal homogeneous state will be an administrative tyranny, and its rulers will be comprised of an administrative class which undoubtedly will have its own hierarchical structure.

In his Second Inaugural Address, delivered on January 20, 2005, President George W. Bush made the startling announcement that, "it is the policy of the United States to seek and support the growth of democratic movements and institutions in every nation and culture, with the ultimate goal of ending tyranny in our world."

"In a world moving toward liberty," Bush predicted, we should have "complete confidence in the eventual triumph of freedom ... because freedom is the permanent hope of mankind ... the longing of the soul." While "history has an ebb and flow of justice," the president concluded, "history also has a visible direction, set by liberty and the Author of Liberty."

Some observers have pointed out that the president's vision of "ending tyranny in our world" is utopian and dangerous. If, as one prominent political philosopher cogently observed, "tyranny is a danger coeval with political life,"[5] then ending tyranny in the world will require a radically transformed human nature in which human beings have been liberated from all desire to rule. President Bush, however, has occasionally expressed the belief that, "evil in some form will always be with us."[6] Here, Bush seemed to confirm the political philosopher's view and perhaps concedes that tyranny is as much a part of the "longing of the soul" as freedom.

This concession, however, is not a central theme for President Bush. He seems to have an unbounded faith in the purposefulness of History – its "visible direction" – and the ultimate purpose of the "Author of Liberty." The goals of History and the purposes of God here seem to be one and the same. If liberty is an intrinsic desire of human nature, so too, he believes, is democracy – the only regime appropriate to liberty.

President Bush's desire to eliminate tyranny in the world will not succeed until that human desire to rule has been exorcised from the human soul. And that desire, as the political philosopher has wisely prophesized, is a permanent part of the human soul that no utopian speculation – no dream of global unity – can erase.

The dream of global unity – that is, a universal homogeneous state of free and equal persons – is the greatest of all deceptions, because the goals to be achieved seem to be so lofty and noble that any means can be justified if they tend to the realization of such goals, including global terrorism. But we must remind ourselves that the human capacity for self-deception is almost unlimited.

Bush did not seem to realize that it would require a universal tyranny to end tyranny in the world. Tyranny itself cannot be eliminated because the desire to rule will remain a permanent feature of the human soul. This grand delusion animated his enthusiasm for the Arab Spring and regime change in the Middle East. It caused untold misery, the displacement and death of untold civilians, the revival of ancient tribal animosities, and religious persecution, among a host of other evils. I am sure Bush and his neoconservative supporters and advisers still believe their reckless interventions were noble ventures to fulfill the human soul's longing for freedom by replacing tyranny with democracy. I do not deny that the human soul longs for freedom, but a prudential recognition of that fact does not demand this kind of utopian – and utterly reckless – commitment to ending tyranny in the world.

These assumptions about human nature and the historical fate of democracy inspired Bush's enthusiasm for the Arab Spring. Democracy, he thought, is easy to establish in souls longing for freedom, as it is endorsed by both History and Providence. Bush thus expressed "universal values" similar to those later expressed by Macron in his commemoration speech. Indeed, it can be fairly and accurately said that Bush had more in common with Macron on the issue of the nation-state and nationalism than he did with President Trump.

## IS DIVERSITY OUR STRENGTH?

For many years Progressives have asked us to believe something incredible: that the most important and admirable aspect of the American character is defined only by its openness and unlimited acceptance of diversity. A devotion to republican principles, republican virtue, the habits and manners of free citizens, and self-reliance would be impermissibly exclusive – and, thus, impermissibly American. The universal homogeneous state only recognizes openness, acceptance and devotion to diversity as virtues. It must, therefore, condemn exclusivity as its greatest vice. It is the nation-state that insists on exclusive citizenship and immigration policies that impose various kinds of restrictions. Openness, as a political virtue, inevitably inclines to the support of open borders, and it would be utterly surprising to learn that the advocates of openness and diversity are unaware of this.

Our Progressive politicians and opinion leaders proclaim their commitment to diversity almost daily, chanting the same refrain: "diversity is our strength." This is the gospel according to political correctness. But how does diversity strengthen us? Is it a force for unity and cohesiveness, or is it a source of division and contention? Does it promote the common good and the friendship that rests at the heart of citizenship, or does it promote the racial and ethnic tribalism that prevents most of the world from making constitutional government a success? We are used to hearing talk about the various stakeholders and group interests, but not much about what the nation has in common. When is the last time anyone in Washington referred to the common good? Greater diversity inevitably means that we have less in common, and the more we encourage diversity, the less we honor the common good.

Any honest observer can see that diversity is the solvent that dissolves the unity and cohesiveness of a nation. We should not be deceived into thinking that proponents of diversity do not understand the full implications of their advocacy; any nation that believes that diversity is its strength has already made the decision to dissolve itself. Anyone can see today that the nation is dissolving – its unity lost, with tribes, races, ethnicities, and various other identity groups competing for superiority. However, diversity *is* the strength of the universal homogeneous state, using diversity to dispense with the common good which supports constitutional democracy and the nation-state.

Diversity, of course, marches under the banner of tolerance; it is, in reality, a bastion of intolerance. It enforces its ideological liberalism with a fanaticism driven by political correctness, the most ingenious (and insidious) stratagem for suppressing freedom of speech, religion, and political dissent ever invented. It is insidious because it is self-imposed, and practiced with a kind of moral fanaticism or religious fervor that is particularly attractive to the young and their sophisticated enablers.

Political correctness could have been stopped dead in its tracks over three decades ago, but Republicans refused to kill it when they had the opportunity. In the 1980 presidential election campaign, Reagan promised to end Affirmative Action by rescinding the executive order issued by Lyndon Johnson that had created it. This promise was warmly received by the electorate, but President Reagan failed to deliver his promised repeal. Too many Republicans had become convinced that they could use Affirmative Action to their advantage, using the largesse associated with racial class entitlements to attract minorities to their party. By signing on to the regime of political correctness, Republicans were never able to mount an effective opposition to its seemingly irresistible advance.

Today, any Republican charged or implicated with racism – however tendentious, outrageous, implausible, exaggerated, or false the charge or implication may be – will quickly surrender, often preemptively. This applies equally to other violations of political correctness: homophobia, Islamophobia, xenophobia, genderphobia, transphobia, and a host of other so-called irrational prejudices. After all, there is no rational defense against an "irrational fear," which is what the various phobias are alleged to be. Republicans have rendered themselves defenseless against political correctness, and the establishment wing of the party doesn't seem particularly concerned, as they frequently joined the chorus of Democrats in denouncing President Trump's alleged violations. Only Trump seemed undeterred in his determination to resist the tyrannical threat that rests at the core of political correctness.

No nation-state can survive by deliberately adopting a policy of "diversity." National unity must be the counter to those liberal (and conservative) Progressives who would propel us into the universal homogeneous state.

There is nothing fated about the global state or the universal person. Nations make choices; they are not simply swept along by the dialectic of History. Contrary to the assurances of George W. Bush – who, no surprise, quickly became a fierce Trump opponent – freedom is not fated. Freedom is not easy simply because the human soul might yearn for it. Every free nation knows that, as is inscribed on one of our nation's monuments (if it survives our current hysteria), "freedom is not free." A nation that cannot

THE UNITED STATES IN CRISIS

control its borders and distinguish between citizens and aliens is no longer a sovereign nation. A nation that is no longer sovereign will not be free for long.

## TRUMP AT THE UNITED NATIONS

In September 2019, President Trump gave a speech to the United Nations that was undoubtedly designed to be a reply to Macron. "The future does not belong to globalists," he told the dedicated globalists at the UN,

> The future belongs to patriots. The future belongs to sovereign and independent nations who protect their citizens, respect their neighbors, and honor the differences that make each country special and unique.

In this rousing defense of nationalism, patriotism, and the nation-state, Trump clearly held up the United Kingdom – still struggling at the time to complete Brexit, its separation from the European Union – as a warning: "If you want democracy, hold on to your sovereignty."

It is astounding that the land of Hobbes and Locke would voluntarily cede its sovereignty to the EU. It does not mitigate the United Kingdom's error that it did so voluntarily and by indirection. Trump could have added that sovereignty once lost – or even diminished – is rarely regained. It is unclear that the UK will ever regain its complete sovereignty even if Brexit succeeds. This was Trump's warning to all nation-states, and it should not be taken lightly. It will, however, be ignored or condemned as advancing all the evils associated with nationalism by irrepressible Progressives, for whom all "universal values" are threatened by the existence of sovereign nations.

President Trump, however, was never driven by such utopian speculations; he touted the sovereign nation's role in preserving peace. The nation can defend itself against tyranny, but it cannot eliminate it. "The free world must embrace its national foundations," he declared.

> It must not attempt to erase them or replace them... If you want freedom, take pride in your country.... And if you want peace, love your nation. Wise leaders always put the good of their own people and their own country first.

That was Trump's warning to a world whose ruling elites believe that the trajectory of History – the dialectic of History – will inevitably lead to the homogeneous world state. Trump understood, however, that the nation-state is the only form of political organization that has ever sustained constitutionalism, freedom, and the rule of law, and that these essential features of democracy have never been found in any form of global government.

Near the end of his speech at the UN, Trump delivered a parting shot across bow of Macron's global ship of state:

> Liberty is only preserved, sovereignty is only secured, democracy is only sustained, greatness is only realized, by the will and devotion of patriots. In their spirit is found the strength to resist oppression, the inspiration to forge legacy, the goodwill to seek friendship, and the bravery to reach for peace. Love of our nations makes the world better for all nations.

President Trump's presidential campaigns in 2016 and 2020 clearly emphasized the importance of the nation-state and citizenship. There cannot be a nation-state without sovereignty, which means, above all, control over who is allowed to become citizens and control over borders. Open borders – the goal of ideological liberalism – mean that illegal immigration will become "legal immigration," and the distinction between aliens and citizens will be abolished. This will certainly be the order of the day if ideological liberals gain power.

An interesting writer observed some years ago that,

[i]n the modern world, sovereignty has been closely associated with constitutional government, at least in the
sense that constitutional governmental has only been
achieved in sovereign states. And it is only in the modern
practice of constitutional government that guarantees of
personal liberty have been combined with political struc-
tures capable of sustaining stable democracy.[7]

This was precisely the message of President Trump's UN speech:
the sovereignty of the nation-state is the surest way to guarantee
the rights and liberties of citizens. In particular nations, citizens
share a common good and have unique privileges and immunities. The Declaration of Independence announces that America
has become a "separate and equal" nation, dedicated to promoting the "safety and happiness" of the people. The happiness of
the people provides the ground of friendship that is the basis of
citizenship; this can only be found in particular nations that are
separate and sovereign. No one can be a "citizen of the world."
The phrase itself is a simple contradiction. To be a citizen is to
belong to a particular regime, and a particular regime cannot be
a universal regime. The "universal person" is no less a post-mod-
ern fantasy than the "universal citizen."

## CHAPTER TWO

# WHY CITIZENSHIP MATTERS

IN THEIR PUSH to establish global government, Progressives seek to abolish not only the nation-state and nationalism, but also its principal component: citizenship. Citizenship is, by nature, exclusive. Citizens share the privileges and immunities and the rights and liberties of particular sovereign nations. From the progressive point of view, any kind of exclusivity is anachronistic, because progressives insist that the dialectic of History is inevitably moving toward global institutions and universal citizenship. The universality of rights points to universal citizenship or, more precisely, "universal personhood." The advent of the borderless world, they assert, will render citizenship superfluous. The dialectic of History has consigned citizens and citizenship to an irretrievable past, as human rights, properly understood, cannot be exclusive rights dependent on the protection of separate sovereign nations with different systems of government and different concepts of what constitutes human rights.

Even otherwise sensible scholars believe that history is somehow an independent and irresistible force in human affairs as they scramble to be on the "right side of History" lest they be denounced in the future for their shortsightedness, or worse, risk accusations of ex post facto offenses against political correctness. Professor Linda Kerber, a distinguished historian at the University of Iowa, asked this question more than twenty years ago at the Organization of American Historians: "Do we need citizenship?

We are embedded in postnational and transnational relationships that may be reconstructing the meaning of citizenship out of recognition."[1]

Professor Kerber's discussion focused mainly on American citizenship and how the nationalism that informed it failed to deal with the issues of slavery, race and ethnic relations, gender issues, class, refugees and a host of other issues involving citizenship. The implication throughout was that nationalism and the nation-state, and not just the form it took in the United States, was always ill-equipped to deal with citizenship because the bundle of issues intrinsic to citizenship continually provoked questions of universal rights. Those issues, Kerber argued, were more suitable for a transnational or global rights context; the nation-state was no longer adequate. Progressivism had always held that the dialectic of History was inevitably moving toward universal politics and away from the nation-state. Hence Professor Kerber's question of whether citizenship itself had become an anachronism in a postnational world that she believed had already arrived. From this point of view, President Donald Trump's attempt to restore national sovereignty was simply reactionary; it was an attempt to defy the fated course of History. His attempt cannot succeed because it is impossible to defy the gods of the Historical dialectic.

But, of course, the Founders of America did not worship the gods of the Historical dialectic. They were inspired by the "Laws of Nature of Nature and of Nature's God." The Laws of Nature are permanent and do not evolve; they are not subject to the "dialectic of History." The Declaration of Independence supplied the authoritative principles upon which the authority of the Constitution itself rested; the Declaration supplied the ends or purposes for which the Constitution furnished the means.

## DEFINING CITIZENSHIP

One curious (but understandable) feature of the Constitution is that, while it refers to citizens, it does not define citizenship. The Constitution specifies that, in order to be eligible for membership in the House of Representatives, a candidate must be a citizen for seven years and twenty-five years of age. Eligibility for the Senate is nine years of citizenship and thirty-five years of age. To be eligible for the presidency, however, an individual must be,

> a natural born Citizen, or a Citizen of the United States, at the time of the Adoption of this Constitution; neither shall any person be eligible to that Office who shall not have attained to the Age of thirty five years, and have been fourteen Years a Resident within the United States. (Art. 2. Sec. 1, Cl. 5).

The first definition of citizenship did not find a place in the Constitution until the Citizenship Clause was ratified in 1868, as the first sentence of the Fourteenth Amendment. As a practical matter, state citizenship determined federal citizenship with respect to eligibility to constitutional offices. Anyone who was deemed to be a citizen of one of the ratifying states was considered to be a citizen of the United States.

The Preamble to the Constitution notes that, "We the people of the United States ... do ordain and establish this Constitution for the United States of America." It is important to note that the people create the Constitution; the Constitution did not create the people. Article VII proclaims that the Constitution was,

> done in Convention by the Unanimous Consent of the States present the Seventeenth Day of September in the Year of our Lord one thousand seven hundred and Eighty seven and of the Independence of the United States of America the Twelfth.

The twelfth year of American independence points to the Declaration of Independence. That is when the American people became a people, and the Declaration is the authority that sanctioned their act in creating the Constitution. America declared itself a "separate and equal" nation in 1776 appealing to the "Laws of Nature and of Nature's God," which dictate that the "just powers" of government must be derived from "the consent of the governed."

The Constitution – and its ultimate ratification by conventions elected by the people for that purpose – was an act of the sovereign people. In *Federalist* 39, James Madison wrote that "the fundamental principles of the Revolution" required a "strictly republican" form of government and if the proposed Constitution departed from the republican form, Madison warned, it should be rejected by the people. The "principles of the Revolution," of course, are the principles of the Declaration which Madison cites again at the virtual center of *The Federalist* as, "the transcendent law of nature and of nature's God, which declares that the safety and happiness of society are the objects at which all political institutions aim." There is no doubt that the Founders believed that the principles of the Declaration of Independence serve as the foundation upon which the authority of the Constitution rested.[2]

When the Constitution specifies that the eligibility for the presidency required "a natural born citizen" who is at least thirty-five-years old, the framers were aware that there were no thirty-five-year-old citizens born in America after the date of the Declaration. Indeed, in 1789 there were no natural born citizens. The framers therefore specified that any thirty-five-year-old citizen at the time of the adoption of the Constitution who had been a resident of the United States for fourteen years was eligible. The fourteen-year requirement points to the Declaration. The first natural born president (born in the United States after the Declaration) was, by my calculations, Martin Van Buren (born in

1782); he served as the eighth president of the United States, from 1837–1841.

The origin of the "natural born" requirement for the president is said to reside in the fact that the president was to be the Commander-in-Chief of the armed forces, and that a guard against any foreign influence in the office was imperative. John Jay wrote to George Washington early in the Constitutional Convention, asking,

> whether it would be wise and seasonable to provide a strong check to the admission of Foreigners into the administration of our national Government; and to declare expressly that the Command in Chief of the American army shall not be given to nor devolve on, any but a natural born Citizen.[3]

Jay, subsequently one of the authors of *The Federalist*, called for a "strong check" against "Foreigners" in any part of the administration of "our national" government and an absolute prohibition against foreigners becoming head of the American army. Foreign meddling was always a present fear, and there was even some worry that a monarchical plot might be underfoot. Madison expressed strong reservations at the Constitutional Convention about having the legislative branch elect the executive because, "[t]he Ministers of foreign powers would have and make use of, the opportunity to mix their intrigues & influence with the Election."[4] Although Madison's principal objection to the legislature's election of the executive stemmed from his concern about separation of powers, his trepidations about foreign interference in the election of the president were real. In any case, Jay's recommendation was adopted by the Convention with remarkably little debate – yet no definition of natural born citizen was included in the text of the Constitution.

## *WHO ARE CITIZENS?*

Founders of new regimes face a unique dilemma: they are not citizens of the new regime that they create. Creators are always superior to their creations, and it would be unjust to make them obey the laws they have created. In a word, the founders of the laws are a law unto themselves. When a new regime comes into existence – when it is founded – it has no citizens. The citizens of a new regime have to be created along with the regime. Citizens are thus not natural. They are conventional; they are created by the laws.

In the third book of the *Politics*, Aristotle presents something of a paradox: in book one he had famously claimed that the *polis* or political community existed by nature but, in the later book, he insists that citizens exist only by convention. How is that possible? The *polis*, of course, cannot exist without citizens, but Aristotle says there are no citizens by nature.

It is law, not nature, that defines citizenship. Citizens are relative to the regime. The good citizen of a democracy will not be a good citizen in an oligarchy, nor will he be a good citizen in a monarchy. Being a citizen of a democracy requires different habits and manners – different virtues – than those required of a citizen in a monarchy.

Democratic citizens are expected to take responsibility for their freedom and participate in the deliberation and offices of the regime. It is for this reason that citizenship is most applicable to a democratic regime in which rotation in office is routine, as citizens rule and are ruled in turn. Citizens in a monarchy never participate in rule or deliberation; they are used to obeying the commands of the law without participating in the making of the law.

Aristotle points out that custom or convention usually defines a citizen as the offspring of parents who are both citizens, sometimes requiring two or three generations of citizen ancestors. But these customs cannot account for the first citizens or for the founders of regimes themselves. Those who become citizens of a new regime did not descend from citizen parents; they became citizens by the operation of law.

In book three of Plato's *Republic,* Socrates tells the Guardians that they are the "earth born," the *geganai,* who simply sprang from the earth and have an indissoluble attachment to it as natural born citizens. They have thus committed no injustice in occupying their land because they have displaced no previous occupants in their spontaneous growth from the earth. But unlike these *geganai* from Plato's myth of autochthony, every people in the world has come from somewhere else and has, therefore, committed the injustice of displacing previous occupiers. There are no exceptions to this fateful fact, and there are, I say, no natural born citizens or "first occupier" citizens in the world – not even Native Americans, who themselves came from other places.

Our American confusion is highlighted when we speak of "naturalizing citizens" – i.e., making citizens "natural" by law. We say someone is a "natural born citizen" if they have been born within the geographical limits of the United States. This is, we are told, something we inherited from the English common law. But this is the common law, not nature, and those considered citizens under the common law as "natural-born" are not citizens by "nature," but by law. We have laws to "naturalize" foreigners we wish to make citizens – but these laws cannot make them "natural citizens" any more than the common law can make citizens "natural born." It is a simple fact that there are no citizens by nature – citizens are not born, they are made. No citizens are earthborn like the *geganai* of the myth in Plato's *Republic.* Questions of citizenship will always provoke questions about the principles and character of the regime because citizens, as Aristotle rightly argued, are relative to the regime.

## THE FOURTEENTH AMENDMENT
## AND THE DEFINITION OF CITIZENSHIP

There was no constitutional definition of citizenship until the adoption of the Fourteenth Amendment in 1868: "All persons born or naturalized in the United States and subject to the jurisdiction thereof, are citizens of the United States and of the State wherein they reside."

The Supreme Court decided in *United States v. Wong Kim Ark* (1898) that the framers of the Citizenship Clause of the amendment intended to adopt the common law of *jus soli* as the foundation of American citizenship. As we will see in the next chapter, Justice Horace Gray argued that the plain language of the Citizenship Clause is compelling. But as we argue, the phrase "subject to the jurisdiction" is completely alien to the common law, so a plain reading of the language would lead us to wonder what the common law has to do with the Fourteenth Amendment's Citizenship Clause.

Justice Gray makes another puzzling argument: since the plain language of the Citizenship Clause clearly points to a foundation in the common law, it is not necessary to consider the congressional debates and the intentions of the framers. The odd and utterly puzzling feature of this argument is that the author of the Citizenship Clause did not mention the common law when he introduced it in the Senate on May 30, 1866 – and not a single principal supporter of the clause, nor anyone who spoke in its favor, ever mentioned the common law, or Blackstone, or Sir Edward Coke, the author of the opinion in the *Calvin's Case* (1608) which was first case to codify British subjectship.

This deafening silence might well have attracted Justice Gray's attention, but he was so intent on basing American citizenship on the common law, that no contrary evidence seemed to deter him. He did note that William Blackstone's *Commentaries on the Laws of England* was the authoritative source for the common law at the time of the Founding, and that the framers of the Constitution were well acquainted with that seminal work. That was certainly a true observation, but it is simply a non-sequitur to argue that because framers were well acquainted with the works of Blackstone they wrote a common law constitution and intended citizenship in the new regime to be based on the English common law.

As I hope to prove, in this chapter and the next, the evidence is overwhelming: A common law understanding of American citizenship runs contrary to an understanding of the framers of the Fourteenth Amendment and of America's founding principles and, in fact, was explicitly rejected by America's most authoritative statement of fundamental principles, the Declaration of Independence, when the American people declared themselves, "Absolved from all Allegiance to the British Crown."

Under the common law, subjects of the king – the situation of Americans until 1776 – owed "perpetual allegiance to the king" as a debt of gratitude for being born within his protection. This debt could never be thrown off or cancelled without the permission of the king. The Declaration proclaimed what the common law expressly disallowed; King George III resisted by force of arms until he was forced to recognize America as an independent, separate, sovereign nation in the Treaty of Paris in 1783. None of the commentators on the common law – Coke or Blackstone – ever mentions "citizen" or "citizenship," always "subjects" and "subjectship." Under the common law, there were no citizens, only subjects, who owed allegiance by the accident of birth. The Declaration of Independence was a revolution: it transformed subjects into citizens where citizenship was based on consent, not the accident of birth.

Blackstone had described "birth-right subjectship" in these terms:

> Natural allegiance is such as is due from all men born
> within the king's dominions immediately upon their birth,
> For, immediately upon their birth, they are under the

king's protection ... Natural allegiance is therefore a debt of gratitude; which cannot be forfeited, cancelled, or altered, by any change of time, place, or circumstance, nor by any thing... For it is a principle of universal law, that the natural-born subject of one prince cannot by any act of his own, no, not by swearing allegiance to another, put off or discharge his natural allegiance of the former: for this natural allegiance was intrinsic; and primitive, and antecedent to the other.[5]

Blackstone readily admits that "birth-right subjectship" is an inheritance from the "feudal system," since it derives from the, "mutual trust or confidence subsisting between the lord and vassal." And Blackstone continues, "[b]y an easy analogy the term of allegiance was soon brought to signify all other engagements, which are due from subjects to their prince."[6] It is significant, as I will argue, that Blackstone never uses the word "citizen" in his four-volume commentary. It is always "subject," and "subjectship." Clearly, under the common law, there are no citizens, only subjects.

Justice Gray's opinion in *Wong Kim Ark* provoked a vigorous dissent written by Chief Justice Melville Fuller that was joined by Justice John Harlan. Fuller's principal argument was that whatever in the common law that was incompatible with principles of the Declaration was null and void from the beginning. This is certainly true of the feudal institution of birthright subjectship. I believe the Chief Justice's dissent is unanswerable.

Gray's majority opinion has remained unchallenged, despite the many erroneous legal and historical assumptions that it indulges. It is my express intention to argue that this opinion is not only contrary to the intentions of the framers of the Fourteenth Amendment but, as Chief Justice Fuller points out in his dissent, contrary to the first principles of the Founding as well.

Modern scholars seem to believe that there only two choices

for determining citizenship: *just soli*, citizenship by place of birth; or *jus sanguinis*, citizenship by descent. But the American Founders relied on neither of these; rather, the ground of citizenship was the social compact principles embodied in the Declaration of Independence. No one can be ruled or become a citizen without his consent. The common law of subjectship was involuntary and perpetual. The Declaration announced that the American people were absolved of all allegiance to the British crown. This was an explicit repudiation of the common law of subjectship. It is impossible to believe that the same American people, having repealed the common law, at one and the same time adopted this feudal relic as the basis for the citizenship of the new republican regime that was being created.

## A NEW REGIME AND A NEW CITIZENSHIP

The Declaration translated subjects into citizens by making consent the basis of citizenship. The Declaration posits the "consent of the governed" as the basis for the "just powers" of government. This means that the active participation of citizens in their own governance will replace the passive "subjectship" that was at the heart of "*jus soli.*" James Wilson, signer of the Declaration and the Constitution and later a member of the Supreme Court, certainly had Blackstone in mind when he wrote in 1793 that, "[u]nder the Constitution of the United States there are citizens, but no subjects."[7] American citizenship, in his opinion, did not rest on the common law.

In 1776, all Americans were British subjects owing perpetual allegiance to the King. Americans were well aware that the Declaration was in defiance of the common law. The King, of course, refused to accept this American effrontery and opposed it by force of arms. It was only when American insolence directed at the dictates of the English common law was ratified by the victory at Yorktown and recognized by the King in the Treaty of Paris in 1783 that America became an "equal and separate" nation – a sovereign nation, taking its place "among the Powers of the Earth." Americans were now recognized by their former king as free citizens of an independent, sovereign nation. Too many commentators would have us believe that Americans remained subjects – or as Justice Gray insisted in his majority opinion in *Wong Kim Ark*, that for purposes of constitutional analysis, "subject" and "citizen" are convertible terms. Gray was following the commentator James Kent, who had argued that although,

> the term citizen seems to be appropriate to republican freemen, yet we are, equally with the inhabitants of all other countries, subjects, for we are equally bound by allegiance and subjection to the government and law of the land.[8]

Gray here is agreeing to a palpable sleight of hand on Kent's part. "Subjects" and "citizens" are not convertible terms any more than monarchy and republic are convertible forms of governments simply because they are both sovereign. This is a doctrine that would please Thomas Hobbes, who argued that since all regimes were sovereign the differences between regimes forms were negligible. But this was an argument that was rejected by the American Founders.

The framers of the American Constitution were acutely aware of regime differences; they certainly never confused monarchies with republics, or subjects with citizens. Any form of government not derived from the consent of the governed – or in which the "just powers" of government were not derived from the sovereignty of the people – was not a legitimate form of government, because it did not conform to the principles of the "Laws of Nature and of Nature's God." The framers insisted that the only form of government appropriate for Americans was one that was "strictly republican," because, as Madison wrote in *The Federalist*, no other form would be reconcilable with the genius of the people of America; with the fundamental principles of the Revolution; or with that honorable determination which animates every votary of freedom to rest all our political experiments on the capacity of mankind for self-government.[9]

In the center of this enumeration is the recognition that only the republican form of government is compatible with the "fundamental principles of the Revolution." If the principles of the Revolution are the point of departure, then *eo ipso* "birthright ligeance" must be rejected as the basis for American citizenship. We cannot too often remind ourselves that the Declaration proclaims the American people to be, "Absolved from all Allegiance to the British Crown." This is a clear and authoritative rejection of the common law. The case that the framers of the Constitution and the framers of the Fourteenth Amendment adopted the English common law of birthright ligeance simply cannot be sustained.

The American Revolution created a new country based on new regime principles. Since citizens are relative to the regime, a new regime requires new citizens. When the Declaration of Independence proclaimed that Americans had dissolved their allegiance to King George III and rejected the common law rule of involuntary and perpetual subjectship, there were no American citizens. They had to be created. Subjects had to be transformed into citizens. The general outlines to govern this transformation had been delineated in the Declaration of Independence. Citizenship rested on consent. No person could become a citizen without his consent, and every person who consented to become a citizen of the new regime also consented to fulfill the obligations of citizenship.

This was social compact in which citizens agreed to be ruled and delegated limited portions of their sovereignty to government for the protection of their "safety and happiness." No one could become a citizen without his consent and no one who was unwilling or unable to fulfill his obligations as a citizen would be acceptable as a citizen. But the implementation of these principles was not so easy. How to transform Americans from subjects to citizens in practice was baffling; the theory was simple, the practice – especially because of the existence of separate states – made the implementation difficult and uniformity impossible.

James H. Kettner succinctly described the situation when he remarked that,

> [t]he dissolution of the imperial bonds in 1776 gave the authority to admit members to the community to the individual state governments. Americans charged that the long list of grievances committed by George *III* amounted to a withdrawal of his protection over them, and they declared themselves absolved of their former allegiance as British subjects. In the king's place there now stood thirteen independent states, each claiming the fidelity of the inhabitants remaining within its bounds. The new states not only sought the loyalty of their present inhabitants and former fellow subjects; they also extended a broad welcome to the foreign-born.[10]

The states decided the question of allegiance and citizenship differently, but there were common themes. Anyone who participated in taking up arms against Britain was automatically considered a citizen whether alien or native born. Others who were native born – including loyalists to the king who remained – were given a period of election, specifying a date certain, to determine whether to declare allegiance to the newly constituted state. In the 1830 US Supreme Court case, *Inglis v. The Trustees of Snug Harbor*, Justice Smith Thompson summarized the general issue by writing that the,

> right of election must necessarily exist in all revolutions like ours, and is ... well established by adjudged cases. The

only difficulty that can arise is to determine the time when the election should have been made.*

In general, prior state cases had determined that the right of election must take place within a reasonable time and, in any case, must have occurred after July 4, 1776, and before the date of the first exercise of legislative sovereignty on the part of the new state governments, and in no case later than 1783, the date of the Treaty of Paris. Anyone remaining after that date was considered to have given tacit consent, and thereby to have acquired the obligations of allegiance to the new government.

The first government of the United States, the Articles of Confederation, was not ratified until 1781. It contained no power for the Federal Government to define or regulate citizenship. As previously mentioned, the Constitution of 1789, although referring to citizens, did not define who were citizens. Both the Articles and the Constitution, however, contained a "comity clause," which in Article IV of the Constitution of 1789 reads: "The Citizens of each State shall be entitled to all privileges and Immunities of Citizens in the several States." This language clearly implies a national citizenship.

Joseph Story saw the connection between the comity clause in Article IV and the fact that the exclusive power of naturalization is lodged in the national government. "It is obvious," Story wrote in his *Commentaries on the Constitution of the United States*,

---

* Inglis v. Trustees of Sailor's Snug Harbor, 28 U.S. (3 Pet.) 99, 122 (1830) (Thompson, J.) Justice Thompson does note that "I am not aware of any case in the American courts where this right of election has been denied, except that of Ainsley v. Martin, 9 Mass. 454. Chief Justice Parsons does there seem to recognize and apply the doctrine of perpetual allegiance in the fullest extent. He then declares that a person born in Massachusetts, and who, before the 4th of July, 1776, withdrew into the British dominions and never since returned to the United States, was not an alien; that his allegiance to the King of Great Britain was founded on his birth within his dominions, and that that allegiance accrued to the Commonwealth of Massachusetts as his lawful successor." I will have occasion to discuss this case in greater detail in due course.

that, if the citizens of each state were to be deemed aliens to each other, they could not take, or hold real estate, or other privileges, except as other aliens. The intention of this clause was to confer on them, if one may so say, a general citizenship; and to communicate all the privileges and immunities which the citizens of the same state would be entitled to under the like circumstances.[11]

In essence, the citizen of every state is a citizen of every other state, at least with respect to privileges and immunities of the state to which he happens to relocate or where he may be a temporary sojourner.

It is important to notice that the language to Article IV is mandatory: "shall be entitled." One wonders why Story seems reluctant ("if one may so say") to reveal that the framers of the Constitution introduced the idea of national citizenship in such an evasive manner. It reveals that citizenship is emphatically a national issue intimately connected with the nation's sovereignty, hence its connection to Congress's exclusive power to enact uniform rules of naturalization.

But many observers at the Convention must also have realized that this clause was also a potential time bomb in so far it would allow free black citizens of states to travel to slave states and demand federal protection for the same privileges and immunities of the citizens of the slave states. Any demand for a straightforward definition of citizenship at the Convention not only would have exacerbated delicate issues of the federal relationship; it would also have provoked a debate about race and slavery that would have almost certainly broken up the Convention. The southern states had threatened on several occasions to withdraw and create a separate nation which they euphemistically called a "slaveholding republic."

This was probably the real reason that "citizen" and "citizenship" could not be defined in the Constitution until the slavery issue was resolved. Federalist leaders knew that, without a compromise on the issue of slavery, there would be no agreement on a strong national government, and without a strong national government there would be little prospects of ever ending slavery. The provisions dealing with slavery were not a part of the principles of the Constitution; rather, they were compromises: temporary departures from principles to secure the acceptance of the southern states. Thus, the compromises were in the ultimate service of the principles themselves. As Abraham Lincoln was to say later, the Constitution, read in the light of the principles of the Declaration of Independence, had put slavery in, "the course of ultimate extinction." Those compromises – which, to be clear, were protections for slavery – were, in the long run, prudent measures in the interest of slaves. No slave could be expected to understand how it was in his interest to continue in slavery, but leading Federalists understood that without a strong national and united government slavery would probably continue into the distant future.

What about immediate emancipation? After all, slavery surely violates the principles of the Declaration of Independence, and the American people are dedicated to those principles and agreed that those principles were authoritative for the Constitution. But the framers of the Constitution faced a tragic dilemma. Although the people accepted the principle that "all men are created equal" as the dictate of the "Laws of Nature and of Nature's God," they were unwilling to consent to the immediate emancipation of slaves. It is easy, of course, to agree in principle, to accept that slavery is unjust and in contravention of the laws of nature. But when racial prejudice and private interests are at stake, principles are easily forgotten or postponed. It is difficult, if not impossible, to translate political theory into political practice. "I know the better and I do the worse," is something that all human beings have experienced. In democracies, all political action must exist within the horizon of political opinion or consent. Democratic statesmanship removes as much evil as possible while possible without destroying the basis in public opinion for removing further evil in the future. If the framers had abolished slavery all at once at the time of the Founding, it would have been without the consent of the governed, which is the ground and foundation of legitimate government itself. It would therefore have purchased the freedom of the slaves at the expense of enslaving the free by acting without their consent. The statesmanlike alternative was to create the constitutional ground that would eventually lead to emancipation when public opinion was eventually led to accept its necessity. Once the principal was established that slavery was unjust, then moral appeals could be made for eventual emancipation and opinion could be rallied in support of the principle.

In June of 1857, Lincoln gave a speech criticizing the Dred Scott opinion. In his majority opinion, Chief Justice Taney had made the incredible assertion that had the writers of the Declaration of Independence actually believed that, "all men were created equal," they would have emancipated slaves immediately. Since they did not do so, it must be inferred, Taney argued, that such honorable men would not have acted with such hypocrisy. When read by themselves, the words "all men are created equal" are capacious enough, "to embrace the whole human family" but, judged by the action of its authors, there is no reason to conclude that they included Blacks of African descent in that language – otherwise, they would have freed the slaves immediately, regardless of the consequences. Had these honorable men believed that Blacks were created equal without acting to free the slaves immediately, they would have been vulnerable, as Lincoln noted, to the base charge of "hypocrisy." In Taney's mind, this was unthinkable. Their actions speak louder than their words, and the actions of the authors, not their words are decisive in determining what they meant. Lincoln deftly points out the illogic of Taney's argument: he has "proven" that the Declaration did not includes whites by the mere fact that not all whites were equalized all at once.

I think the authors of that notable instrument intended to include *all men*, but they did not intend to declare all men equal in *all* respects. They did not mean to say all men were equal in color, size, intellect, moral developments, or social capacity. They defined with tolerable distinctness, in what respects they did consider all men created equal – equal in "certain inalienable rights, among which are life, liberty, and the pursuit of happiness." This they said, and this they meant. They did not mean to assert the obvious untruth that all were then actually enjoying that equality, nor yet that they that they were about to confer such it immediately upon them. In fact, they had no power to confer such a boon. They meant simply to declare the *right*, so that the *enforcement* of it might follow as fast as circumstances should permit. They meant to set up a standard maxim for free society, which should be familiar to all, and revered by all. It was to be constantly looked to, constantly labored for. Even though it would never be perfectly attained, it would be constantly approximated, spreading and deepening its influence and augmenting the happiness and value of life to all people of all colors everywhere.

The assertion that "all men are created equal" was of no practical use in effecting our separation from Great Britain; it was placed in the Declaration for future use. Its authors meant it to be a stumbling block to those who might seek to turn a free people back onto the hateful path of despotism.[12] It is now proving itself to be such an impediment to tyrannical government, thank God.

As Lincoln rightly noted, there was "no such power" to equalize blacks and whites – or even all whites. They only power possessed by the framers of the Declaration was to create a "standard maxim," a guide for future enforcement of the principle of equality.

Lincoln also pointed out factual errors in Taney's decision, most notably those referred to in Justice Benjamin Curtis's *Dred Scott* dissent. Curtis successfully rebutted Taney's claim that blacks of African descent were no part of the people who framed and adopted the Constitution when he pointed out that free blacks,

in at least five of the States ... had the power to act, and doubtless did act, by their suffrages, upon the question of its adoption. It would be strange, if we were to find in that instrument anything which deprived of their citizenship any part of the people of the United States who were among those by whom it was established.[13]

Curtis also points out that Taney's categorical demand that the framers would have freed the slaves all at once had they believed "all men" included blacks ignores the fact that the framers did not have the power to accomplish such a feat. In short, it ignores the necessary element of statesmanship in the framers' view of republican politics. "My own opinion," Justice Curtis asserts,

is, that a calm comparison of these assertions of universal abstract truths, and of their own individual opinions and acts would not leave these men under reproach of inconsistency; that the great truths they asserted on that solemn occasion, they were ready and anxious to make effectual, wherever a necessary regard to circumstances, which no statesman can disregard without producing more evil than good, would allow; and that it would not be just to them, nor true in itself, to allege that they intended to say that the Creator of all men had endowed the white race, exclusively, with the great natural rights which the Declaration of Independence asserts.[14]

Lincoln had declared in his critique of the *Dred Scott* decision that, "I could no more improve on McLean and Curtis, than [Senator Stephen Douglas] could on Taney."[15] McLean, of course, had also filed a stinging rebuke of Taney's majority decision which, as much as Curtis's dissent, emphasized the Declaration and founding principles. But while it is evident that Senator Douglas was unable to improve on Taney's woefully flawed analysis – his impossible contention that the phrase "all men are created equal" meant only that British subjects in America were equal to British subjects born and resident in Great Britain at the time converts

Taney's "categorical imperative" into high comedy[16] – although it is clear to any intelligent observer that Lincoln did improve substantially on the dissents of McKlean and Curtis.

Although it has not been widely recognized, Chief Justice Taney in his opinion in *Dred Scott* was an early exponent of the "historical consciousness" that later became an important element of the historicism that is at the center of Progressivism. He argued that the framers of the Declaration were merely expressing the dominant opinions of their day. Even the greatest statesmen are unable to transcend the orthodoxies of their time. Thus an accurate assessment of their work must take into account the climate of opinion in which they operated. Nothing they did or said was revolutionary or transcended the authoritative opinion of their time.

Taney was thus an early adherent of historicism. All thought is relative to the era in which it is produced, even the thought of the most far-sighted thinkers and statesmen. The Declaration was not revolutionary, nor was it a call for revolution, even though its framers might have deluded themselves into thinking it was. The language of the Declaration, when considered in the context of prevailing opinion shows, Chief Justice Taney asserts,

> that neither the class of persons who had been imported as slaves, nor their descendants, whether they had become free or not, were then acknowledged as part of the people, nor intended to be included in the general words used in that memorable instrument.[17]

Taney described what he thought the regnant opinion of the founding era was: this class of persons for more than a century, he avowed, has,

> been regarded as beings of an inferior order; and altogether unfit to associate with the white race, either in social or political relations; and so far inferior, that they had no rights which the white man was bound to respect;

and that the negro might justly and lawfully be reduced to slavery for his benefit.[18]

The enlightened opinion of the civilized world at that day regarded blacks of African descent as mere articles of property to be, "bought and sold, and treated as an ordinary article of merchandise and traffic wherever a profit could be made by it."[19] And since these were not only the most enlightened opinions of that day – but shared by the most sophisticated and learned people – they were undoubtedly shared by the framers of the Declaration who, regardless of their capacity to speak the language of the timeless truths of natural right, were merely reflecting the most powerful orthodoxies of their time. Their belief that the principles of the Declaration were applicable to all men everywhere and always was simply a self-willed delusion.

## MEN ARE NOT CREATED EQUAL
## IN ALL RESPECTS

The equality of the Declaration must be understood in terms of natural right or "the rights of human nature." It is a self-evident truth that "all men are created equal" because no one is so superior by nature to occupy the position of a natural ruler, having been marked by God or Nature's God to rule. It must also be acknowledged that it is also a "self-evident" truth that "all men are not created equal in all respects." As Lincoln noted, men are not created "equal in color, size, intellect, moral developments, or social capacity." They are, however, created equal in the natural rights to "life, liberty, and the pursuit of happiness."

None of the qualities in which men are created unequal establishes a claim to rule others by nature. Size or power may give one the power to rule, but not the right to rule by nature. Inequality in intelligence might seem to qualify as a natural claim to rule based on superior intelligence or wisdom. As Jefferson noted in a famous letter, however, "because Sir Isaac Newton was superior to others in understanding, he was not therefore lord of the person or property of others."[20] Natural inequalities in the capacity for moral or social development, which most certainly exist, are subject to the same criticism.

The most puzzling quality Lincoln mentions is inequality of "color." Color, of course, is an accidental feature of the human persona; it is not part of the essence of human nature. Certainly, there cannot be a natural inequality of color, such as exists with respect to size, intelligence, and moral and social capacity. Distinctions of color are arbitrary, having no connection with nature or natural right, and Lincoln's mention of color first in the list seems to emphasize this. Inequality of "color" can exist only by convention – never by nature – as slavery itself exists only by law or convention and never by nature or natural right. From a slightly different point of view, one could say that the inequality between God and man is so great that whatever inequalities exist between human beings would be insignificant (indeed non-existent) in the eyes of God. It could therefore be easily argued that the equality doctrine of the Declaration is one of natural law as well as divine law (the Laws of Nature and of Nature's God").

Taney's argument wholly misunderstood the founders' view of statesmanship. Lincoln argued that the "abstract truth at the core of the Declaration served no practical purpose in effectuating independence from Great Britain." In fact, Lincoln says, it was not placed in the Declaration for that reason but for future use as a "standard maxim" or a goal to be attained. Once it was accepted, the Declaration placed moral demands on all Americans. How those demands were to be met and at what speed had to be determined by wise statesmen within the constraints of public opinion at the same time that that it attempts to lead public opinion ever closer to the fulfillment of its highest aspirations.

Today's abandonment of the principles of the Declaration have opened the door to identity politics, where the first concern of the law is the racial, ethnic and gender class one happens to identify. Race and ethnicity, gender and transgender, and sexual orientation in its various guises have all been given special recognition for purposes of the Constitution and law. The concept behind the Declaration – the equal protection of equal rights of individuals regardless of class or caste – has given way to a rebirth of the caste and tribal systems of the past, where rights are conditioned by claims of tribal and caste privileges instead of the privileges and immunities of citizenship. This development is often praised as progress. But anyone with the slightest understanding of the meaning of progress understands that the retreat to tribalism is not progress. But, if we are convinced that citizenship is truly anachronistic, and global citizenship is utterly utopian and unworkable, tribalism may be the only alternative. This alternative, of course, will require new gods representing new tribes. Any reasonable person knows that these gods will not be benevolent gods.

## *LYNCH V. CLARKE (1844)*

*Lynch v. Clarke,* an 1844 decision of the New York Chancery Court, was cited as authoritative by Justice Gray in his majority opinion in *Wong Kim Ark.* Constitutional commentators continue to believe that his reliance on the case was proper, even though Justice Gray made important departures from Assistant Vice-Chancellor Lewis Sandford's opinion. And Sandford's opinion itself had failed to demonstrate that the common law has always been the basis of American citizenship.

The facts of the case are as follows: Julia Lynch was born in the City of New York in the spring of 1819. Her parents were British subjects domiciled in Ireland who came to America in 1815 as sojourners with no intention of remaining or establishing domicile. They returned to Ireland in the summer of 1819, taking Julia with them. She remained in Ireland until she returned to America at age 15 in 1834. She was never naturalized. In 1833, her uncle had died intestate – that is, without having made a will. The question was whether Julia was an American citizen by birth – and, therefore, eligible to inherit her uncle's property – or a British subject, incapable of inheriting under New York state law.

American citizenship, Sandford noted, "is a national right or condition and does not pertain to the individual states."[21] The guard against "different and discordant rules for establishing the right of citizenship in [the] future," was the power conferred on Congress to pass uniform rules of naturalization for the entire U.S.[22] The Court duly notes that the Constitution does not explicitly confer on Congress the power define citizenship, but implies that power as a necessary implication from Congress' plenary and exclusive power to pass laws on naturalization.

Thus, Sandford argued, the question before the court – the citizenship of Julia Lynch – is a national issue rather than one pertaining to the State of New York. The very "reason of the thing" renders it "a matter of national concern," resting, "with the powers of Congress under the Constitution. Citizenship ... is a political right which stands not upon the municipal law of any one state, but upon the more general principles of national law."[23]

Sandford then moves to a rather loosely argued proof that, after the Revolution in 1776, the states had adopted the common law as the basis for citizenship. "When our national independence was declared, the citizens of this and the other states were subjects of Great Britain. Upon the Revolution, they were at liberty to continue their allegiance to the crown and retire from the country or to remain and adhere to the independent states." He concluded that "the common law was ... the law of all the states."[24]

We have already seen in the discussion of the Supreme Court decision in *Inglis v. The Trustees of Snug Harbor* – decided fourteen years before *Lynch* – that, with one exception, the states after the Revolution relied on social compact principles, not the common law, in deciding the issue of citizenship. Inhabitants were given a deadline or a period in which consent or election had to be exercised as to whether to retain allegiance to the British crown or to choose allegiance to the newly free state government. The requirement of consent was, of course, no part of the common law, but a requirement of social compact reasoning embodied in the principles of the Declaration of Independence. The Declaration, we recall, had repealed the common law of subjectship and replaced it with "consent" as the ground of citizenship. This, not the common law, was the rule that was applied by the states.

The leading case for New York, although receiving only one casual reference in Sandford's opinion despite heavy reliance by counsel, was *Jackson v. White* (1822). It relied on consent either "tacitly or expressly" as the ground for citizenship after allegiance to "the old government" has been "dissolved." Chief Justice John C. Spencer wrote that,

> I think it cannot be doubted, that when a people, from the sense of the viciousness of a government under which they have lived, are driven to the necessity of redressing themselves, by throwing off the allegiance which they owed to that government, and in its stead erecting a new and independent one of their own, that such of the members of the old government only will become members of the new as choose voluntarily to submit to it. Every member of the old government must have the right to decide for himself, whether he will continue with a society which has so fundamentally changed its condition. For, having been incorporated with a society under a form of government which was approved, no one can be required to adhere to that society, when it has materially and radically changed its Constitution. Every member submitted to the society as it was, and owed obedience to it, while it remained the same political society. When it devests itself of that quality, by an entire new institution of government, it cuts the knot which united its members, and discharges them from their former obligations.[25]

Spencer thus gave a thorough explanation of the meaning of the Declaration's statement that the free and independent states of America, "are Absolved from all Allegiance to the British Crown." In arguing that "it cuts the knot" and "discharges them from their former obligations," he means that renouncing their allegiance is the same as renouncing the common law, as the common law forbids discharging allegiance without the permission of the king.

We recall once again that the Declaration's central charge against the king that, "he has abdicated Government here, by declaring us out his Protection and waging War against us." The king has abdicated government and the people in turn have abdicated their allegiance. The withdrawal of allegiance is a rejection of the common law and "perpetual subjectship." We must always bear in mind throughout that there is no such thing as common law citizenship. Spencer mentions that the principles governing the "absolution" were expounded "in a very satisfactory manner" by Chief Justice M'Kean in *Chapman's* case, an opinion we will explore shortly.

Chief Justice Spencer also cites a United States Supreme Court decision handed down in 1808 in which a person born in England before the Declaration of Independence (and who had always resided there) was ineligible as an alien to inherit under Maryland law from an American citizen. Justice William Johnson, writing for the Supreme Court, argued that the person who sought to inherit "never owed allegiance to our government" because of "his never having been a party in our social compact" and therefore always remained an alien.[26] Spencer concludes his social compact analysis by remarking,

> that a new form of government, and a new organization of the political society took place, cannot be denied; and hence the case occurred in which every member of the old society had a right to determine upon adhering to his old allegiance, and withdraw himself, or to abide among us,

and thus tacitly, or expressly, yielding his assent to the change, and becoming a member of the new society.[27]

Thus, the new society finds its legitimacy in the consent of the governed, not a debt of gratitude. This is clearly the language of social compact; it is the language of the Declaration of Independence, not that of the common law.

In *Jackson*, the Chief Justice faced something of a dilemma. As he observed, the Declaration was passed on July 4, 1776 and adopted by the Convention of Delegates in New York on July 9. Committees and temporary bodies took immediate charge of public safety and no organized government emerged in New York until April of the following year. In the interim period, there was only an "imperfect and inchoate government" which had had been "called into existence by the necessity of the case, and was continued until the people could deliberate and settle down upon a plan of government calculated to secure and perpetuate their liberties."[28]

What causes the particular dilemma is that the case involved a charge of treason against a British officer, Major Edmonston, who had been captured and paroled in New York in the interim period in which there was "no organized government." The question was whether an "imperfect and inchoate government" could support a charge of treason. As it turns out, however, Major Edmonston was sent out of the country as "a dangerous and disaffected man" one or two months after the date of the Declaration and "prior to the institution of any regular form of government." He later claimed American citizenship in order to inherit the estate of his brother who had become a New York citizen. Considering his departure before the establishment of the new constitution, it "appears manifest," the Chief Justice concluded, that he cannot be considered as having thrown off his allegiance to [his] former government, and that consequently, he never became a member of the new government, but remained a British subject."[29] All of his actions indicate his continued allegiance to the British crown. Thus, there was no consent, either express or implicit, to become a citizen of New York. He had retained his "perpetual allegiance" to the king; he had not entered the social compact of the new constitution adopted in 1777 which defined the citizenship of New York.

This is a far cry from the decision in *Ainsley v. Martin* which, as we noted above, the US Supreme Court said in *Inglis v. Trustees of Sailor's Snug Harbor* (1830) was the only state case that held that upon the abdication of King George III, "allegiance accrued to the commonwealth [of Massachusetts] as his lawful successor."[30] Massachusetts, Chief Justice Theophilus Parsons ruled in *Ainsley,* had adopted the common law rule. Again, contrary to Vice-Chancellor Sandford, we must be mindful that the United States Supreme Court in 1830 had – fourteen years before *Lynch* – remarked that only Massachusetts, not *all* states, had adopted the common law rule of "citizenship."

In *Jackson*, Chief Justice Spencer praised the opinion of the Chief Justice of the Pennsylvania Supreme Court, Thomas M'Kean, in the case of *Respublica v. Chapman* (1781). The Chief Justice relates that. "a general convention, elected by the people, met on the 15th day of July, 1776, for the express purpose of framing a new government ... and the constitution which they eventually adopted, was incontrovertibly a dissolution of the government, as far as related to the powers of Great Britain..." There was subsequently, the court notes, "a revival of the laws, passed the 28th of January, 1777," concluding that,

> [w]e may ... fairly infer from the general tenor of the act, that those who framed it, thought the separation from Great Britain worked a dissolution of all government, and that the force ... of the common law and statute law of England, was actually extinguished by that event.[31]

With the rejection of the common law, the new ground of allegiance and obligation is derived from social compact. "The cases which have been produced upon the present controversy," M'Kean writes,

> are of an old government being dissolved, and the people assembling, in order to form a new one. When such instances occur, the voice of the majority must be conclusive, as to the adoption of the new system; but, all the writers agree, that the minority have individually, an unrestrainable right to remove with their property into another country; that a reasonable time for that purpose ought to be allowed, and, in short that none are subjects of the adopted government, who have not freely assented to it.[32]

Consent is thus the legitimate ground for civil society: no one can be ruled without his consent. There can be no involuntary subjectship as under the common law. Those who do not consent must be free to leave with their property and be given a reasonable time to make a decision. This was the way the states decided to handle the transition to freedom after the Revolution. Only Massachusetts decided the common law devolved automatically from the king.

## EXPATRIATION AND THE COMMON LAW

The issue of expatriation in state law is another issue that leads to questions about whether or not Sandford was correct in his assertion that, after the American Revolution, "the common law was ... the law of all the states."[33] He introduces the subject by remarking that,

> the much vexed question of the right of expatriation, was pressed into the argument; and it was urged that if we adopt the common law rule of allegiance by birth, we must also adopt that of perpetual allegiance, which it was

said, has been repudiated in this country. The authorities in our courts are much divided upon that question, and many which are of great weight, are adverse to the right to expatriate.[34]

It is remarkable that the Declaration's unequivocal repudiation of "perpetual allegiance" is dismissed with a casual "it is said," and that unnamed "authorities in our courts ... of great weight" are on this question "adverse to the right to expatriate." Sandford duly mentions that Pennsylvania, Virginia and Kentucky all recognized the right to expatriate, but curiously concludes that this "diversity prevailing in the colonies and states prior to 1789," is evidence that, while perpetual allegiance did not prevail in the national government, the rule of allegiance which prevailed in all the colonies and states is "a convincing argument that such rule became the national law."[35] The diversity that existed in the states cannot be used as evidence of unanimity.

Expatriation and perpetual allegiance are incompatible and the three states that permitted expatriation did not accept the common law of perpetual allegiance either. If the British common law of allegiance which was explicitly repudiated by the Declaration had, somehow, been miraculously resurrected by the silence of the Constitution, then it was a much transformed common law which no longer contained the essential element of perpetual allegiance. The Vice-Chancellor does not indicate that he understood that the principles of the Declaration revolutionized the common law's idea of involuntary and perpetual allegiance by making allegiance voluntary and based on consent. As we have demonstrated above, this was clearly understood those who wrote the post-Revolutionary state constitutions based on social compact principles.

The right of expatriation, although not always expressed in explicit terms, was always implicit in social compact theory. In the *Summary View of the Rights of British America* (1774) – which might be described as the first version of the Declaration – Jefferson described expatriation as a natural right that every person possesses of leaving the country where chance and not choice has placed him. Chance is accident; choice implies reason and natural right. Jefferson often referred to the natural right of expatriation. When he was a member of the committee to revise the legal code for Virginia, appointed in 1776 he proposed a bill proclaiming the "natural right, which all men have of relinquishing the country, in which birth, or other accident may have thrown them, and seeking subsistence and happiness wheresoever they may be able or may hope to find them."[36]

In his opinion, the Vice-Chancellor often cites James Wilson as an authority. But Wilson can hardly be said to support the *Lynch* holding on the common law. He certainly does not support Sandford's casual dismissal of the natural right to expatriation. In fact, Wilson agreed with Jefferson when he stated in his "Lectures on Law" that,

> every man being born free, a native citizen, when he arrives at the age of discretion, may examine whether it be convenient for him to join in the society, for which he was destined by his birth. If, on examination, he finds, that it will be more advantageous to him to remove into another country, he has a right to go, making to that which he leaves a proper return for what it has done in his favour, and preserving for it, as far as it shall be consistent with the engagements, which his new situation and connections may require, the sentiments of respect and attachment.

As his first authority, Wilson cites Locke's *Second Treatise* rather than Blackstone on the common law.

> Tis plain, [says Locke] by the law of right reason [meaning the laws of nature] that a child is born a subject of no country or government. He is under his father's tuition and authority, till he comes to the age of discretion; and

then he is a freeman, at liberty what government he will put himself under, what body politick he will unite himself to.

The natural right of expatriation is thus essential to an understanding of social compact – yet nothing could be further from the common law. Locke and social compact is the authority for the Declaration and the Constitution, not Blackstone and the common law.[37]

The natural right to expatriation, of course, cannot be exercised to escape the obligations to society that have already been incurred or to avoid arrest or punishment for crimes. When an individual consents to be governed for the protection of his rights and liberties, he simultaneously incurs the obligation to protect the rights and liberties of his fellow citizens. No one who is unwilling or unable to join in the mutual protection of the equal rights of the equal citizens who consent to be ruled can be a member of this new civil society. Those who are unable or unwilling to incur the obligation of society remain in the state of nature with respect to the newly formed society, whose members are defined by the obligations they owe to one another.

Once this first society is formed, a government is established which is granted powers to be exercised for the sole purpose of securing the "safety and happiness" of those who have consented. The Declaration specifies the terms and even the form of the government: the people must regularly renew their consent to be governed through regularly scheduled elections; there must be a separation of powers; and most importantly, the people always reserve the right to withdraw their consent when the government either by design or incapacity fails to protect the rights and liberties of the people.

This withdrawal of consent is known as the right of revolution, the ultimate expression of the people's sovereignty, which the Declaration describes as both a right *and a duty*. The right of revolution is thus the right the guarantees every other right. Limited constitutional government is possible only because the people's ultimate expression of sovereignty is a constant reminder that elections are successful substitutes for revolution as a control on government. The failure to accept the legitimacy of an election, as the South did in 1860, is an attempt to dissolve the sovereignty of the people, in the same way the American people dissolved their allegiance to the British crown in 1776. But in 1860, the South did not have justice on its side. Its defense of slavery could not be defended by appeals to the "Laws of Nature and of Nature's God."

When a child is born into a society based on compact, his allegiance follows that of his parents until he reaches the age of consent. Until that time, his parents' ability to reason serves as the substitute for the child's lack of ability; the parents have a duty to act in the best interest of the child. When the child reaches the age of consent, he is presumed to be able to make reasoned decisions. At this point, he can elect to remain a citizen in the society of his birth, thus continuing to enjoy the protection of his rights and liberties the society affords. Once he has made the election, his new allegiance means that he has now incurred obligations as a fully participating citizen.

The other election available upon reaching the age of consent is, as we have just seen, to exercise the natural right to expatriation and find another country that will allow him to emigrate where he believes his happiness will be better served. The country of his birth – if it is based on social compact and natural right principles – has an obligation to allow the person to choose expatriation. The recognition of the natural right of expatriation, as the authors of the Declaration of Independence were keenly aware, was inherent in the logic of social compact.

Assistant Vice-Chancellor Sandford ignores or misunderstands the principles of social compact. His arguments that the Constitution rests on the common law are unconvincing. Sandford argues that the requirement that the president must be a natural born citizen or a citizen at the time of the adoption of the Constitution "contains a direct recognition of the subsisting common law principle."[38] Sandford does not quote some relevant portions of the eligibility clause that we have previously discussed, which bear repeating here. The parts that are left out are that the president must be (1) at least thirty-five years old; and (2) a resident of the United States for fourteen years.

The fourteen-year requirement coincided with the Declaration of Independence, the date also specified in Article VII of the Constitution as, "the independence of the United States of America." Thus, the conclusion is inescapable: *natural born citizens* were those born in the United States after the Declaration of Independence. In 1789, there was no one who was thirty-five years old who was a natural born citizen, but there were thirty-five year olds who had resided in America for fourteen years since 1776. Thus, Sandford's confident conclusion the "[t]he only standard which then existed, *of a natural born citizen*, was the rule of the common law, and no different standard has been adopted since,"[39] was simply mistaken.

Not to put too fine a point on the matter, "natural born citizen" is not a common law term because the common law recognizes *subjects* and not citizens. We will have occasion later to discuss the claim advanced by James Kent in his *Commentaries on American Law* and accepted by Justice Gray in his majority opinion in *Wong Kim Ark*, that subjects and citizens are merely convertible terms[40] – a claim that I believe the framers of the Declaration and the authors of the *Federalist* would have treated with utter contempt. In the Constitution, "natural born citizen" means anyone born in the United States after the date of the Declaration of Independence. I am confident that the evidence is clear: the common law rule was not adopted by the Constitution. "Natural born citizen" was defined by the principles of the Declaration of Independence.

Sandford goes further: "The Constitution of the United States, like those of all the original states ... presupposed the existence and authority of the common law. The principles of that law were the basis of our institutions." It is true that the common law was not adopted *in toto*, but that part that was inapplicable was rejected, and new rules for the regulation of government prescribed. But, according to Sandford, it is clear, "our ancestors ... founded their respective state constitutions and the great national compact upon its existing principles, so far as they were consistent and harmonious with the provisions of those constitutions."[41] What is required to make them "consistent and harmonious," he doesn't venture to say.

Sandford does point out, however, several common law terms that made their way into the Constitution and the Bill of Rights. These include treason, cases in equity, attainder, writ of habeas corpus, right to petition, capital crimes, trial by jury, bail, fines. All of these (and others) are common law terms or concepts incorporated into the Constitution of 1789 and most of them were left "to stand upon the same footing that they previously were, the principles of the unwritten common law" – "as a matter of course, without doubt or question."[42] This last clause is pure hyperbole, as I will endeavor to explain.

I is certainly true that the terms and concepts Sandford mentions appear in the Constitution. But do they appear *as common law terms*? We have argued that the Declaration was the authoritative source for the Constitution, and the authoritative source for the Declaration was "the Laws of Nature of Nature's God." With regard to bills attainder, trial by jury, the writ of habeas corpus, the right to petition government for a redress of grievances, the prohibition of excessive bail and other provisions that use common law language involving individual rights, it is questionable that they were included in the Constitution because America was the heir of the historical experience of the common law. Rather, these rights – although in the form of the common law – were viewed, not as part of America's common law heritage, but as natural rights, the dictates of the Law of Nature. The Constitution protects the right of habeas corpus, which certainly revealed its usefulness in the course of English history in the struggle against tyranny. The prohibition against ex post facto was another tool against English tyranny.

Were these prohibitions (which emerged from unique English history) simply the heritage of America and accepted as the rights of Englishmen? Or were these rights that were valid everywhere and always in the struggle against tyrannical rule? These were not just the historical rights of Englishmen, but the natural rights of all men who struggle against tyrannical government.

For Americans, the rights that appear in the Constitution and the Bill of Rights are natural rights, not historical rights or rights that have emerged exclusively from English historical development.[43] They may have appeared in the Constitution in the language of the common law, but the common law had been transformed into natural right by the Declaration and the Constitution. That was the core of the American Revolution: historical rights were transformed into natural rights grounded in the law of nature. The rights in the Constitution are no longer anchored in the common law, but the natural right principles of the Declaration. The use of common law language scattered throughout the Constitution does not mean that the Constitution itself is a common law document. As we have demonstrated, its principles rest on the natural right principles of the Declaration. Sandford's argument is a simple non-sequitur.

Near the conclusion of his opinion, Sandford cites "legal and judicial authorities on this subject."[44] The first is Chancellor Kent, who, the Vice-Chancellor alleges,

> follows Blackstone in his division of the inhabitants of our country into *aliens and natives*. And he says: "Natives are all persons born within the jurisdiction of the United States;" and "an alien is a person born out of the jurisdiction of the United States." The exceptions which he makes, do not affect the present question.[45]

Turning to the text of James Kent's *Commentaries on American Law*, one finds something surprising about what Kent says it means to be born "within the jurisdiction of the United States." Lecture XXV "Of Aliens and Natives," deals with "the rights and duties of citizens in their domestic relations" most of which are "derived from the law of nature." First, it is necessary to distinguish between natives and aliens:

> Natives are all persons born within the jurisdiction of the United States. If they were resident citizens at the time of the declaration of independence, though born elsewhere, and deliberately yielded to it an express or implied sanction, they became parties to it, and are to be considered as natives; their social tie being coeval with the existence of the nation.

July 4, 1776 was the first date that someone could have been born within the jurisdiction of the U.S. All other residents were born somewhere else, even if within the territory that eventually became the United States. If they elected to remain, either by explicit or implicit consent, they became members of the new society and "natives." Those born before the declaration who "voluntarily withdrew into other parts of the British dominions, and never returned" did not owe allegiance to the new government. Kent's reasoning follows that of the state courts that we previously rehearsed; these courts acknowledged the importance of the Declaration of Independence as the date at which jurisdiction vested and the importance of voluntary consent as necessary to the establishment of allegiance. As for the definition of "Alien," Kent simply says "[a]n alien is a person born out of the jurisdiction of the United States," but notes that "[t]here are some exceptions, however to this rule, by the ancient English law..." Sandford had mentioned that none of the exceptions mentioned by Kent "affect the present question." But Kent does mention the exception created by the statute of 25 Edward III. Stat. 2., which "declared, that children thereafter born without the ligeance of the king, whose father and mother, at the time of their birth, were natives, should be entitled to the privileges of native subjects..."[46] Thus the English law would seem to determine that someone like Julia Child – born to parents who were British subjects owing allegiance to the king, who always intended to return to Ireland – was a British subject at birth. Sandford was clearly aware of this possibility, but his legal prowess was not deterred. "I believe," he stated, "it to have been the common law of England that children born abroad of English parents, were subjects of the crown. The statute, 25 Edward III., st. 2, *De natis ultra mare*, appears to have been declaratory of the old common law."[47]

And here is where a bit of legal legerdemain takes place.

If such were the common law, it was in force in the colonies, and was one of the rights which the citizens of the United States retained and still hold under the Constitution. The provisions in the acts of Congress of 1790, 1795 and 1802, to secure these rights to children born abroad, were in this view a superabundant caution.[48]

What the act of 1802 specifically commands is that children born abroad to American citizens are to be considered American citizens and not birthright citizens of the countries where they are born if that country holds to birthright citizenship or subjectship. Sandford thus believes that the U.S. has adopted the common law and extended it to children of American citizens born abroad. If a child is born in England of American parents, for example, he will have been born within the protection of the king and therefore be a birthright subject of the king. Yet if born after the passage of the 1802 law, that child will be an American citizen as well; he will be both perpetual subject and citizen. This creates something of an anomaly: the common law does not recognize dual citizenship (or subjectship), but in this instance the child is clearly a dual citizen (or at least a subject/citizen having dual allegiances), as are the thousands of British subjects who had been naturalized as American citizens over the years – those who were birthright subjects of the king and to whom they owed perpetual allegiance that could not be put off without his permission.

"The policy of our nation," the Vice-Chancellor intones, "has always been to bestow the right of citizenship freely, and with a liberality unknown to the old world. I hold this to be our sound and wise policy still." He claims that America is at a disadvantage. Britain claims as subjects all who are born in her dominions and the children born elsewhere as her subjects as well. But America claims as citizens all who are born in America, but only the children born abroad of Americans who were citizens after 1802, a limited field that "is nearly spent in its operation." So that America, "holding to the common law rule, are subjected to great inequality in this grasping and selfish game." Double allegiance, as in the case of Julia Lynch, should not be a deterrent, because it is contrary to common law; many naturalized American citizens of British descent have sworn exclusive allegiance to the United States while still owing perpetual allegiance to the British crown under the English common law which does not recognize the dissolution of perpetual allegiance.

This was possible only because Americans established a different version of the "common law" which, according to Sandford's transmogrification, allows "double allegiance"[49] – something that is emphatically disallowed under the English version. These starkly contrasting and competing views of the common law almost led to war on several occasions before and after the War of 1812, as naturalized American citizens were impressed into the British naval service because they were still "subjects" who "owed perpetual allegiance" to the King of England. The pleas of "double allegiance" or "dissolution of allegiance" fell on deaf ears or were drowned out by shouts of "once a British subject always a British subject." But the Vice-Chancellor's accounts throughout were simply not accurate; no distinctive common law or common law adapted to American circumstances was ever developed in America.

The Vice-Chancellor quotes Justice Joseph Story's opinion in *Inglis v. The Sailor's Snug Harbor* (1830), a case decided by the U.S. Supreme Court which we have already noted, to bolster his account that, after the Revolution, the common law was the law of the states and the United States.[50] However, Story provides no support and, in fact, provides arguments against the holding in *Lynch*. In *Inglis*, the Supreme Court held that the facts of the case were uncontested.

According to Justice Smith Thompson,

> it was the fixed determination of Charles Inglis, the father, at the Declaration of Independence, to adhere to his native allegiance. And John Inglis, the son, must be deemed to have followed the condition of his father, and the character of a British subject attached to and fastened on him also, which he has never attempted to throw off by act disaffirming the choice made for him by his father.[51]

Not being an American citizen, Inglis could not inherit.

Justice Story wrote a separate opinion dissenting from that part of the majority opinion concerning the disposition of the trust. While he didn't decide on the question of the citizenship status of Inglis because he believed the facts were not dispositive, he did agree with the majority opinion about the constitutional grounds on which the decision should be made. We have previously discussed Justice Thompson's majority opinion on the matter of citizenship which was in stark contrast to that of Vice-Chancellor Sandford in *Lynch*. Story's opinion is considerably more comprehensive than Thompson's, but in complete agreement about the constitutional analysis required. Before the Revolution, Story relates, all the colonies were part of the British Empire and "all the colonists were natural-born subjects, entitled to all the privileges of British-born subjects." In each of the colonies there were governments established by the authority of the crown and subordinate to it. The Declaration of Independence,

> proclaimed the colonies free and independent States;
> treating them not as communities in which all govern-
> ment was dissolved and society was resolved into its first
> natural elements, but as organized States, having a pres-
> ent form of government, and entitled to remodel that
> form according to the necessities or policy of the people.

When the dissolution of the political connection between the
Colonies and Great Britain absolved the colonists "from all allegiance to the British crown," the states themselves were not
thrown into a state of nature. The governments of the states were
not dissolved – this, Story asserted,

> would have led to a subversion of all civil and political
> rights and a destruction [of] all laws. Rather the states
> retained their corporate identities and some "proceeded
> to act and legislate before the adoption of any new consti-
> tution, some … framed new constitutions, and some …
> have continued to act under old charters.[52]

There was no question that the perpetual allegiance of the common law had been overthrown. Yet, according to Justice Story,

> [f]rom this perplexing state of affairs, the necessary
> accompaniment of a civil war, it could not escape the
> notice of the eminent men of that day that most distressing
> questions arise … The common law furnished no perfect
> guide, or rather, admitted of different interpretations.

As we have already seen in the cases we have examined, states
relied on consent and social compact principles to determine
allegiance and citizenship. Justice Story acknowledges that,

> [u]nder the peculiar circumstances of the Revolution, the
> general (I do not say the universal) principle adopted was

to consider all persons, whether natives or inhabitants upon the occurrence of the Revolution, entitled to make their choice either to remain subjects of the British crown or to become members of the United States. This choice was necessarily to be made within a reasonable time.[53]

As we have seen, what was reasonable varied from state to state. But in no case could it extend beyond 1783, the date of the Treaty of Paris when the formal acceptance of America as a "separate and equal" sovereign nation was accepted by the British crown. But, on the basis of the decision in *Inglis*, it is clear beyond any possible doubt that the common law of perpetual allegiance subjectship that had been rejected by the principles of the American Revolution was now accepted by the British crown. The allegiance that emerged from the principles of the Revolution was the product of social compact, not the common law. In republican government allegiance is held in trust, not in perpetuity.

## CHAPTER THREE

# THE CASE AGAINST CITIZENSHIP

Before the Coronavirus pandemic gripped the American consciousness in early 2020, America was seized by a pandemic of another kind: a hysteria among the nation's elites over President Donald Trump's immigration policies. The frenzy generated by the progressive-liberal press, Hollywood radicals, progressive politicians (both Democrat and Republican), the minions of the Deep State, academics and law professors was unprecedented.

It was driven, for the most part, by the Trump administration's attempts to curtail illegal immigration by the adoption of a zero-tolerance policy for illegal border crossers; significant restrictions on asylum policies; the use of the National Emergencies Act to shift funds allocated for other purposes to build a border war; the use of the "remain in Mexico" policy for asylum seekers while their claims are evaluated; and the end of the long-standing "catch and release" policy.

But nothing engendered as much hysteria as the president's bare suggestion that, in 2018 – the year of the sesquicentennial of the adoption of the Fourteenth Amendment – the policy of granting automatic birthright citizenship to the children of illegal aliens born in the United States should be ended.

*United States v. Wong Kim Ark* was decided in 1898 and has remained the authoritative interpretation of the Fourteenth

Amendment's Citizenship Clause to this day. The majority decision, written by Justice Horace Gray, held that the clause must be understood in terms of the English common law. The plain language is compelling, Gray argued, and can yield no other result. The Clause reads, "All persons born or naturalized in the United States, and subject to the jurisdiction thereof, are citizens of the United States and the State wherein they reside." The most striking feature of the clause is the fact that the phrase "subject to the jurisdiction" is alien to the common law.

The first case to articulate the grounds for English subjectship was Sir Edward Coke's famous opinion in *Calvin's Case* in 1608.[1] "Ligeance is a true and faithful obedience of the subject due to his sovereign," Coke wrote. "This ligeance and obedience is an incident inseparable to every subject: for as soon as he is born, he oweth by birth-right ligeance and obedience to his sovereign."[2]

Coke's exposition became authoritative for the common law and was used by William Blackstone in his *Commentaries on the Laws of England*, a work that was widely read at the time of the Founding and well known to the framers of the Fourteenth Amendment. Blackstone's account of "birth-right ligeance" in the *Commentaries* was a reprise of Coke's opinion in *Calvin's Case*. He says in a passage we had occasion to quote more fully in the last chapter: "Natural allegiance is such as is due from all men born within the king's dominions immediately upon their birth [citing *Calvin's Case*]. For, immediately upon their birth they are under the king's protection."[3] What is striking about the passages from *Calvin's Case* and Blackstone is the absence of any language implying anything about "subject to the jurisdiction." Rather, the common law speaks of "allegiance," and it would be difficult, if not impossible, to find the word "jurisdiction" associated with "subjectship" in the common law. We must also remind ourselves of the fact that "citizen" or "citizenship" is also alien to the common law.

The framers of the Citizenship Clause intentionally avoided using the word "allegiance" in the clause because they wanted to dispel any idea that citizenship derived from the common law. Thus, Justice Gray's argument in *Wong Kim Ark* – that the plain language must yield a common law result – is demonstrably wrong; it was intended to yield the opposite result. The express intention, as we will show, was to avoid any possible inference that the Citizenship Clause derived any meaning from the common law. During the debate, no one suggested the Citizenship Clause was based on the common law. Justice Gray avers that,

> [d]oubtless, the intention of the Congress which framed and the states which adopted this Amendment of the Constitution must be sought in the words of the Amendment; *and the debates in Congress are not admissible as evidence to control the meaning of those words.*[4]

The reason that Gray wanted to dismiss the importance of the congressional debates is the simple fact that none of the principal supporters of the Citizenship Clause ever suggested that it derived its authority from the common law or that American citizenship was based on the common law. No one mentioned the greatest common law authorities, Sir Edward Coke or Blackstone, or even the common law itself. The chances that these omissions were random cannot be believed, especially if the framers of the Citizenship Clause intended for American citizenship to be based on the common law. If that were the case, they would have no reason to conceal it.

Of course, Justice Gray wanted to confine himself to the text because that was the only chance he had to make a case for the common law understanding – and even there, the phrase "subject to the jurisdiction" proved impossible to square with the common law. And the one foray into the congressional debate that he thought he could use to his advantage turned into a disaster for the cause he championed. Justice Gray didn't seem to realize that the plain text excluded any connection to the common law as much as the congressional debates did.

Justice Gray's decision is not only wrong in its interpretation of the Founding, but also in its interpretation of the intentions of the framers of the Fourteenth Amendment. It should be overruled.

The Citizenship Clause was a late addition to the Fourteenth Amendment. Senator Benjamin Wade, Republican of Ohio, suggested on May 23, 1866, that, given the importance of the amendment's guarantee of privileges and immunities to U.S. citizens from state abridgement, it was imperative that a "strong and clear" definition of citizenship be added to the amendment. He proposed this language: "persons born in the United States or naturalized by the laws thereof."[5] Had this language been accepted by Congress and ratified as the amendment, Justice Gray might have had a better case, although Wade does not say his proposed amendment reflected a common law understanding. In fact, he says that any uncertainty regarding citizenship had been "settled by the civil rights bill" [viz., the Civil Right Act of 1866].

Wade's proposal was referred to the Joint Committee on Reconstruction, and Senator Jacob Howard presented the committee's draft, which became the first sentence of the Fourteenth Amendment. The significant addition to Wade's proposal was the "subject to the jurisdiction" clause. Senator Howard was the floor manager for the amendment in the Senate and, evidently, he and the Joint Committee placed some importance on the addition of the jurisdiction clause. That meant, at a minimum, that not all persons born in the United States were automatically citizens; they also had to be "subject to the jurisdiction" of the United States. His remarks introducing the new language in the Senate have attracted much attention as well as much controversy.

"I do not propose to say anything on that subject," Howard said,

> except that the question of citizenship has been so fully discussed in this body as not to need any further elucidation, in my opinion. This amendment which I have offered

is simply declaratory of what I regard as the law of the land already, that every person born within the limits of the of the United States, and subject to their jurisdiction, is by virtue of natural law and national law a citizen of the United States. This will not, of course, include persons born in the United States who are foreigners, aliens, who belong to the families of ambassadors or foreign ministers accredited to the Government of the United States, but will include every other class of persons. It settles the great question of citizenship and removes all doubt as to what persons are or are not citizens of the United States. This has long been a great desideratum in the jurisprudence and legislation of this country.[6]

When Senator Howard said he regarded the Citizenship Clause as declaratory of the law as it already existed, he was, of course, referring to the Civil Rights Act of 1866, which had been passed over the veto of President Andrew Johnson by a two-thirds majority in both houses less than two months prior to the May 30th debate in the Senate. The author of the Civil Rights Act was Senator Lyman Trumbull, Republican of Illinois, and co-author of the Thirteenth Amendment. The Civil Rights Act provided the first definition of citizenship after the ratification of the Thirteenth Amendment and specified, "[t]hat all persons born in the United States and not subject to any foreign power, excluding Indians not taxed, are hereby declared to be citizens of the United States."

Thus, an overwhelming majority of Congress – on the eve of the debate over the meaning of the Citizenship Clause of section one of the Fourteenth Amendment – were committed to the view that *foreigners* (and aliens) were not subject to birthright citizenship. The Civil Rights Act was palpably clear: not everyone born within the geographical limits of the United States was deemed to be a citizen by birth. If, as many in Congress said, the Citizenship Clause meant to affirm the terms specified in the Civil Rights Act of 1866, not everyone born within the geographical limits of the United States was "subject to the jurisdiction" of the United States. As Chief Justice Fuller cogently observes in his dissenting opinion in *Wong Kim Ark*,

> [t]he act was passed and the amendment proposed by the same congress, and it is not open to reasonable doubt that the words "subject to the jurisdiction thereof," in the amendment, were used as synonymous with the word 'and not subject to any foreign power,' of the act.[7]

Ideological liberals have invented a wholly fabulous interpretation of Senator Howard's speech introducing the Citizenship Clause, maintaining that when he mentions that "foreigners, aliens" are not "subject to the jurisdiction" of the United States he means to include only "families of ambassadors or foreign ministers."* If so, this would be an extraordinarily loose way of speaking: ambassadors and foreign ministers *are foreigners and aliens* and their designation as such would be superfluous. If we give full weight to the commas after "foreigners" and after "aliens," this would indicate a series that might be read in this way: "foreigners, aliens, families of ambassadors, foreign ministers," all separate classes of persons who are excluded from jurisdiction. Or it could be read in this way: "foreigners, aliens, [that is, those who belong to the] families of ambassadors or foreign ministers." I suggest that the natural reading of the passage is the former; the commas suggest a discrete listing of separate classes of persons excluded from jurisdiction. Of course, the debate was documented by

---

* A typical example is Garrett Epps, "The Citizenship Clause: A Legislative History, 60 *American University Law Review*, 331, 381 (2010). "Readily available evidence suggests that the thinkers who guided the Framing [of the Citizenship Clause] saw birthright citizenship as the norm, with the sole exception being children of diplomats." Epps further contends that "this view represented the fruit of the most advanced progressive social thought available to Americans in the year 1866." I submit as a suspicion only that this represents the most advanced progressive liberal thought available to Epps in 2010, not to the Framers of the Citizenship Clause in 1866.

shorthand reporters and not always checked by the speakers, so the issue cannot be settled simply based on the placement of commas.*

Senator Howard had said that everyone born in the U.S. and subject to its jurisdiction, "is by virtue of natural law and national law a citizen of the United States." We have already seen that "national law" clearly refers to the Civil Rights Act of 1866; the reference to "natural law" would have been understood by the members of the Senate as a clear allusion to the Declaration of Independence and social compact. The architectonic theme of the Republicans in the thirty-ninth Congress was to complete the founding by implementing the principles that the framers were compelled to postpone. Thaddeus Stevens, a leading Radical Republican and member of the Joint Committee on Reconstruction, made this point in a speech before the House on May 8,

---

* I once wrote an article published in an online national magazine in which I interpolated Howard's passage in this manner: "This will not, of course, include persons born in the United States who are foreigners, aliens [or] who belong to the families of ambassadors or foreign ministers accredited to the Government of the United States, but will include every other class of persons." The article remained unnoticed for some time until it was rediscovered when President Trump threatened to issue an executive order repealing birthright citizenship. The criticism of my interpolation, which became known as the "bracket war," was vicious. One uninformed critic wrote that the use of the bracketed "[or]" "is based on a blatant lie," and falsifies what "the debates in Congress repeatedly affirmed." Another scribbler, who has the reputation of a constitutional scholar, accused me of "scholarly malpractice" because it "contradicted the unedited text." (See footnote above). The reaction was so intense that the national magazine, without consulting me, edited the text to remove the brackets, even though the editors allowed me to respond in detail to their censorship. The use of the bracket was fully justified when Senator Howard's statement is read in light of the Civil Rights Act of 1866, which explicitly excluded "foreigners" from birthright citizenship and which one of the authors of the Citizenship Clause, Senator Jacob Howard, said the Citizenship Clause was meant to ratify. The bracket war was a small skirmish in a larger war against the liberal orthodoxy that insists against all evidence that the Citizenship Clause excludes only Indians, ambassadors, and foreign ministers. But the attack was vicious and coordinated and succeeded in intimidating one national conservative publication into compliance, admittedly not a difficult task.

1866: "I beg gentlemen," he said "to consider the magnitude of the task that was imposed" on the Joint Committee.

> They were expected to suggest a plan for rebuilding a shattered nation – a nation which though not dissevered was yet shaken and riven ... It cannot be denied that this terrible struggle sprang from the vicious principles incorporated into the institutions of our country. Our fathers had been compelled to postpone the principles of their great Declaration, and wait for their full establishment till a more propitious time. That time ought to be present now.[8]

References to the Declaration as "organic law" were so frequent throughout the debates that one can hardly doubt that the Reconstruction Congress was self-consciously engaged in ratifying a refounding of the regime by embodying in the Constitution the victories that had been won on the battlefields of the Civil War. From this point of view, the Civil War must be understood as the last battle of the Revolutionary War – since only the Reconstruction Amendments bring the Constitution into full compliance with the "fundamental principles of the Revolution."[9]

In listing those who were not subject to the jurisdiction of the United States, Senator Howard seemed to make a glaring omission: he failed to mention Indians. After all, the Civil Rights Act of 1866 had excluded "Indians not taxed" from birthright citizenship. He was forced to clarify his omission when challenged by Senator James R. Doolittle of Wisconsin, who queried whether the "Senator from Michigan does not intend by this amendment to include the Indians;" he thereupon proposed to add "excluding Indians not taxed."[10] Howard vigorously opposed the amendment, remarking that "Indians born within the limits of the United States and who maintain their tribal relations, are not in the sense of this amendment, born subject to the jurisdiction of the United States. They are regarded, and always have been in our legislation and jurisprudence, as being *quasi* foreign nations."[11]

In other words, the omission of Indians from the exceptions to the jurisdiction clause was intentional. Howard clearly regarded Indians as "foreigners, [or] aliens" and thus not "subject to the jurisdiction" of the United States.

This conclusion was supported by Senator Lyman Trumbull who also opposed Doolittle's amendment. Senator Trumbull, chairman of the Senate Judiciary Committee, remarked that "subject to the jurisdiction" meant "subject to the complete jurisdiction" of the United States. This meant, above all, "[n]ot owing allegiance to anyone else." Indians owe allegiance to their tribes and "are not subject to our jurisdiction in the sense of owing allegiance solely to the United States."[12] After much vigorous debate about Senator Doolittle's proposed amendment in the Senate, Senator Howard entered the fray once again supporting Senator Trumbull's statement about jurisdiction:

> I concur entirely with the honorable Senator from Illinois ... Certainly... gentlemen cannot contend that an Indian belonging to a tribe, although born within the limits of a State, is subject to the full and complete jurisdiction. That question has long since been adjudicated, so far as the usage of the Government is concerned. The Government of the United States have always regarded and treated the Indian tribes within our limits as foreign Powers.[13]

Read in light of this statement, the Civil Rights Act, and the authoritative statements by Senator Trumbull in the May 30th debate, can there be any real dispute that "foreigners, aliens" in Senator Howard's opening statement does *not* refer exclusively to "families of ambassadors or foreign ministers" but to "foreigners, aliens" as a separate class?

Determining who was "subject to the jurisdiction of the United States" was a matter of allegiance for Trumbull, Howard, and the principal supporters of the Citizenship Clause. It is for this reason that we have the old common law terms "ligeance" or "allegiance" introduced into the debate to clarify the meaning of "subject to the jurisdiction." The constitutional language "subject to the jurisdiction," Trumbull explained, meant "subject to the complete jurisdiction," by which we understand him to mean not just subject to the laws and the courts – which would be the case for citizens and aliens alike, but something more – owing exclusive allegiance to the United States.[14] Indians owed allegiance, if only partially, to their tribes; foreigners and aliens owed allegiance to other countries. The question that arises, of course, is that if the framers of the Citizenship Clause meant "subject to the jurisdiction" to mean "ligeance" or "allegiance," why didn't they just simply make "owing allegiance to the United States" a qualification of citizenship? Did being "subject to the complete jurisdiction" include "allegiance" in addition to other factors?

During the debate over the Civil Rights Act of 1866, Representative John Bingham of Ohio – himself a leading architect of the Fourteenth Amendment in the House – also spoke of jurisdiction in terms of "allegiance." He averred that the introductory clause of the act "is simply declaratory of what is written in the Constitution, that every human being born within the jurisdiction of the United States of parents not owing allegiance to any foreign sovereignty is ... a natural-born citizen," later refining his statement to simply not "owing foreign allegiance."* We recall that the definition of "citizen" in the act was "all persons born

---

* Ibid., 1291 (Mar. 9, 1866) (Rep. Bingham). Bingham's opinion about allegiance was long held: seven years earlier in debate over the Oregon statehood bill, Bingham queried "[w]ho are citizens of the United States? Sir, they are those, and those only, who *owe allegiance to the Government of the United States...* All free persons born and *domiciled within the jurisdiction of the United States,* are citizens of the United States from birth; all aliens become citizens of the United States only by act of naturalization ..." *Congressional Globe,* 35th Cong., 2nd Sess. 983 (Feb. 11, 1859) (Rep. Bingham) (emphasis added).

in the United States and not subject to any foreign power, excluding Indians not taxed, are hereby declared to be citizens of the United States."

The immediate impetus for the legislation was, of course, to overturn the infamous *Dred Scott* decision, which had held that no black of African descent, slave or free, could ever be a citizen of the United States. This law declared blacks to be natural born citizens. Trumbull, who was also the co-author of the Thirteenth Amendment, believed that emancipation had been sufficient to confer citizenship, but turned to legislation to settle any questions about the issue. Some, however, believed that legislation was insufficient to repeal a Supreme Court decision that had relied on a constitutional interpretation. Others feared that future congressional majorities could simply repeal such legislation. It was this fear that led to the movement to "constitutionalize" the Civil Rights Act.[15]

When introducing the Civil Rights Act, Senator Trumbull said, "I thought that it might perhaps be the best form" to state,

> all persons born in the United States and owing allegiance thereto are hereby declared to be citizens' but upon investigation it was found that a sort of allegiance was due to the country from persons temporarily resident in it whom we would have no right to make citizens, and that that form would not answer.[16]

Trumbull clearly alludes to the fact that, under the common law, temporary allegiance is, "such as is due from an alien, or stranger born, for so long time as he continues within the king's dominion and protection: and it ceases, the instant such stranger transfers himself from this kingdom to another."[17] Thus, the use of common law language in the Civil Rights Act – and, by extension, the Citizenship Clause of the Fourteenth Amendment – would have granted birthright citizenship to children born to those owing only temporary allegiance to the United States. This is, those only in the country for temporary purposes with no intention of remaining or establishing domicile. This would certainly provoke issues of national sovereignty and the nation's control over citizenship. The common law language, as Trumbull realized, was inappropriate even though allegiance was an important element in determining the meaning of "subject to the jurisdiction."

It is abundantly clear that Trumbull intentionally avoided the use of common law language in an effort to dispel any inference that the definition of American citizenship derived any authority from the common law. The same conclusion must be drawn for the Citizenship Clause of the Fourteenth Amendment. We remember that, when introducing the Citizenship Clause, Senator Howard stated clearly that he regarded it as, "simply declaratory of what I regard as the law of the land already." He was obviously referring to the Civil Rights Act of 1866, passed overwhelming by both Houses, just two months prior. As Chief Justice Fuller accurately stated in a previously quoted statement, the Civil Rights Act and the Fourteenth Amendment were actions of the same Congress, "and it is not open to reasonable doubt that the words 'subject to the jurisdiction thereof,' in the amendment, were used as synonymous with the words 'and not subject to any foreign power,' of the act."[18]

## THE EXPATRIATION ACT OF 1868

The Expatriation Act was passed in July 1868, the same month that the ratification of the Fourteenth Amendment was certified. No doubt, the debate over citizenship in the previous Congress had led many Members of Congress to reflect more deeply on the constitutional foundations of citizenship – especially the issue of whether American citizenship was anchored in the English common law. Republican principles compelled the Congress to distinguish American citizenship from the common law in the Citizenship Clause of the Fourteenth Amendment.

Senator Jacob Howard, the principal mover of the clause in

the Congress, was one of the main supporters of the Expatriation Act; his opinion on the matter of citizenship in the Constitution should be given considerable weight. The act was passed by substantial majorities in both houses of Congress. It was debated by many of the same Members who voted to override the president's veto of the Civil Rights Act of 1866 and who also voted to approve the Citizenship Clause of the Fourteenth Amendment. Senator Howard emphasized the declaratory language of the act which stated that, "the right of expatriation is a natural and inherent right of all people, indispensable to the enjoyment of the rights of life, liberty, and the pursuit of happiness." Everyone in the Congress would certainly have recognized this language of the Declaration of Independence. Howard rightly noted that, "the right of expatriation ... is inherent and natural in man as man."[19]

We saw in Chapter Two how Thomas Jefferson, in *Notes on the State of Virginia*, had described expatriation as a natural right that all men possess, "of departing from the country in which chance, not choice has placed them."[20] Choice, as a product of reason, implies natural right; chance is the basis of "accident and force," and is the ground of birthright subjectship and perpetual allegiance as it had become embedded in the common law.

In the debate over the Expatriation Act, the idea of birthright citizenship based on the common law was described by Pennsylvania Democrat Rep. George W. Woodward as an "indefensible feudal doctrine of indefeasible allegiance."[21] This was a frequent refrain of the debate. Rep. Alexander Bailey, a Republican from New York, described birthright citizenship as, "the slavish feudal doctrine of perpetual allegiance."[22] Another Republican, Rep. Frederick Woodbridge of Vermont, one of the principal sponsors of the legislation, provided the most compelling argument. He reasoned that the doctrine of perpetual allegiance,

is based upon the feudal system under which there were no free citizens ... and the individual man [had] no personal rights; and it was from this source and system that Blackstone derived his idea of indefeasible and perpetual allegiance to the English Crown." …. [But] the old feudal doctrine stated by Blackstone and adopted as part of the common law of England, that once a citizen by the accident of birth expatriation under any circumstances less than the consent of the sovereign is an impossibility. The doctrine … is not only at war with the theory of our institutions, but is equally at war with every principle of justice and of sound public law.[23]

Thus, the general sense of the Congress in the wake of the passage of the Citizenship Clause of the Fourteenth Amendment was that the English common law was incompatible with the principles of the Founding. It was clear to these men that citizenship was not based on the "accident of birth," but on "consent"; citizenship did not entail "perpetual allegiance," but held out expatriation as a natural right guaranteed to all citizens.

We have already seen in our discussion of *Lynch v. Clarke* that Vice-Chancellor Sandford considered it something of an innovation on the American version of the common law when some states adopted expatriation. He, of course, knew that expatriation was disallowed by the common law's requirement of "perpetual allegiance." Most importantly – a fact that the Vice-Chancellor refused to acknowledge – the common law of "perpetual allegiance" was incompatible with the first principles of the American regime itself. That was fully acknowledged by the passage of the Expatriation Act, which should be read as companion legislation to the Fourteenth Amendment. The "old feudal doctrine" of Blackstone that grounds citizenship on the "accident of birth" rather than "consent" has been expelled from the United States because it is "at war with the theory of our institutions." Congress understood that, and the framers of the Fourteenth Amendment understood that. Vice-Chancellor Sandford did not. Unfortunately, neither did Justice Gray in *Wong Kim Ark*.

## *WONG KIM ARK*

Wong Kim Ark was born in San Francisco in 1873 to parents who were subjects of the Emperor of China. They "were at the time of his birth domiciled residents of the United States, having previously established and still enjoying a permanent domicil and residence at San Francisco." Wong Kim Ark's parents continued to owe allegiance to the emperor and were incapable by law and treaty with China of becoming citizens of the United States. In 1890, he travelled to China with the intention of returning to the United States and did so in the same year, being readmitted as a native born citizen. He departed again on a visit to China in 1894 with the same intention of returning. Upon his return this time, in 1895, he was refused readmission on the grounds that he was not a citizen of the United States.

The question before the Supreme Court was whether Wong Kim Ark was an American citizen solely by virtue of his birth within the territorial limits of the United States. Justice Gray argued that the Citizenship Clause of the Fourteenth Amendment, no less than other provisions of the Constitution, "must be interpreted in the light of the common law, the principles and history of which were familiarly known to the framers of the Constitution .... The language of the Constitution ... could not be understood without reference to the common law."[24] Gray concludes that "subject to the jurisdiction" meant only to exclude Indian tribes (a category that he admitted was unknown to the common law), and children of Ambassadors and other foreign diplomats born in the United States. Here Gray cited, *inter alia*, Sir Edward Coke's seminal opinion in *Calvin's Case* as his authority. Gray does not provide any argument justifying his position that the common law controls the interpretation of the Constitution. Everyone will, of course, concede that "the principles and history" of the common law "were familiarly known to the framers of the Constitution," but this hardly constitutes proof that they intended the Constitution to be an expression of the common law, unless one chooses to ignore the American Revolution. Gray's argument is a non sequitur.*

Justice Gray follows the argument of *Lynch v. Clarke*, "that there has never been any doubt but that the common law rule was the law of the land" with respect to American citizenship. Justice Gray, however, made one very important exception. Vice-Chancellor Sandford had written that "[u]pon principle, therefore, I can entertain no doubt, but that by the law of the United States, every person born within the dominions and allegiance of the United Sates, *whatever were the situation of his parents*, is a natural born citizen."[25] Justice Gray, however, is very clear in describing the status of Wong Kim Ark's parents: "they were at the time of his birth domiciled residents of the United States, having previously established and still enjoying a permanent domicil and residence at San Francisco."[26] The fact of "permanent domicil," which Gray stresses throughout the opinion, considerably restricts the class covered by the decision in the case. Wong Kim Ark's parents satisfied the elements of domicile, namely, residence and intent to remain. This would not be the case for sojourners who were in the country on a temporary basis

---

* James Wilson, signer of the Declaration of Independence, member of the Constitutional Convention, and a member of the Supreme Court, argued in his famous Lectures on Law delivered in 1790–91, that Blackstone "set out from different points of departure [in] regard to the very first principles of government." Blackstone, he continued, cannot be considered "a friend of republicanism" for the simple reason that he did not support the right of revolution, "the principle of the Constitution of the United States, and of every State of the Union." In other words, Blackstone did not recognize the right of revolution, as did Wilson and other prominent framers, as the right that guaranteed all other rights. Those who debated the Expatriation Act of 1868 echoed Wilson's argument about the principles of the Revolution rejecting the common law as the basis for the Constitution and for interpreting the Constitution. The principles of the Revolution no more supported entail and primogeniture than they did perpetual allegiance; in fact those feudal relics were repealed by that world-historical event. Robert G. McCloskey, ed., *The Works of James Wilson*, 2 vols. (Chicago: University of Chicago Press, 1967), 1:79. These arguments were made *in extenso* in Chief Justice Melville Fuller's dissent.

for business or pleasure with no intention of remaining and who had not established residence. Under the *Wong Kim Ark* ruling, children born to sojourners or others in the country for temporary purposes with no "permanent domicil" would not be entitled to automatic birthright citizenship. After an exhaustive review of cases and authorities, which we will examine in short order, Justice Gray concludes that:

> The 14th Amendment affirms the ancient and fundamental rule of citizenship by birth within the territory, in the allegiance and under the protection of the country, including all children here born of resident aliens, with the exceptions or qualifications (as old as the rule itself) of children of foreign sovereigns or their ministers ... and with the single additional exception of children of members of the Indian tribes owing direct allegiance to their several tribes. The Amendment in clear words and in manifest intent, includes the children born within the territory of the United States, of all other persons, of whatever race or color, domiciled within the United States. Every citizen or subject of another country, while domiciled here, is within the allegiance and the protection, consequently subject to the jurisdiction, of the United States.[27]

A perceptive legal commentator, Justin Lollman, one of the very few to take notice of the importance of the domicile limitations in *Wong Kim Ark*, comments that,

> [t]his statement is perhaps the most significant of the whole opinion. In giving substance to the jurisdictional element of the Citizenship Clause, the Court here interprets the phrase "subject to the jurisdiction" as synonymous with "domicile." If the Court truly believed that every person, all the way down to the temporary sojourner,

was 'subject to the jurisdiction' of the United States, it surely would not have inserted such limiting language into such an important aspect of its opinion.[28]

Summarizing a substantial part of his work, Lollman remarks that there are

> advantages of a parental domicile requirement from a policy perspective. Sound citizenship policy generally seeks, as nearly as possible, to align citizenship status with residency or social ties. Measured against this touchstone, an automatic rule of birthright citizenship is highly over-inclusive. In today's mobile world, place of birth is an increasingly ill-suited metric for predicting whether a person will reside in or develop ties to a political society.... [A] parental domicile requirement offers a rough-and ready means of limiting much of that overinclusiveness.[29]

Wading through the stilted language, this paragraph – which extracts a policy prescription from the *Wong Kim Ark* case – reads like a defense of nationalism and exclusive citizenship. I am not certain that the author or Justice Gray intended that result, but it seems to be a correct analysis after a close reading of the opinion.

As previously mentioned, no subsequent Supreme Court case has revisited the *Wong Kim Ark* decision or, most importantly, ever addressed the issue of whether the Citizenship Clause requires evidence of parental domicile. The executive branch agencies charged with implementing the Citizenship Clause – the Justice Department and the State Department – have determined that all persons born within the geographical limits of the United States are natural born citizens regardless of the status of their parents, with the exception of the children born to ambassadors and foreign ministers.

The common law interpretation of the Citizenship Clause mandated by *Wong Kim Ark* is authoritative; but the "domicile" elements that loomed so large in the case have been ignored even by those who oppose birthright citizenship. Birth tourism would certainly not be available if "domicile" were a requirement; similarly, children born to illegal immigrants who had not established "permanent domicile" would be ineligible for birthright citizenship.*

Children that result from birth tourism and birthright citizenship for children of illegal aliens would also be disallowed under the "subject to the jurisdiction" clause if we properly understood that clause to mean, as its framers did, "not subject to a foreign power" or not owing allegiance to a foreign power.

The Supreme Court has not, except in *dicta*, held that that the children of illegal alien parents are birthright citizens. At this point, I find it difficult to believe there can be any question about the meaning of the Citizenship Clause. "Subject to the jurisdiction" in the Fourteenth Amendment and "and not subject to any foreign power" in the Civil Rights Act are indeed synonymous terms. In the debate over whether Senator Doolittle's amendment that "Indian's not taxed" should be added to those excluded from

---

* Lollman is clear that birth tourists could not meet the burden of the domicile requirements. But he believes that "the parental domicile requirement would not categorically deny citizenship to the U.S.-born children of illegal immigrants." The requirements for domicile are residence with the intent to remain indefinitely. Intent to remain for illegal alien parents, as Lollman points out, would depend on avoiding deportation and therefore conditioned on a future event fraught with such great uncertainty that it would be insufficient ground for forming an intent to remain. Lollman makes a weak argument that because government can legally deprive a person of residence "does not mean that that person is incapable of forming the requisite intent to establish domicile." Lollman cites Plyler v. Doe (1982) as authority for the proposition that illegal entry would not foreclose establishing domicile in a state. But the fantastic hopes of being able permanently to evade extradition and deportation can hardly serve as the legitimate basis for intent to remain, especially when (Plyler to the contrary notwithstanding) the initial entry was illegal and any intentions subsequent to the illegal entry must also be rendered illegal in any rational system. See discussion of Plyer v. Doe in chapter four below.

the Citizenship Clause, Senator Reverdy Johnson explained how the relation of the two acts should be understood:

> Now, all that this amendment provides is, that all persons born in the United States and not subject to some foreign Power – for that, no doubt, is the meaning of the committee who have brought the matter before us – shall be considered as citizens of the United States. That would seem to be not only a wise but a necessary provision.[30]

One of the most egregious misreading of these two congressional actions was made by Professor Garrett Epps, who predictably bends constitutional analysis to serve ideological purposes. The Civil Rights Act and the Citizenship Clause, he asserts, have "different wording," and the meanings of the different acts "must stand on [their] own." Furthermore, the Citizenship Clause

> emerged from a different political situation; it was adopted under different procedures and had different authors, and it was approved by different voting bodies. If its broad wording, which makes no mention of 'foreign powers,' is to be read restrictively, it must be because of something in its text or adoption, not because it is viewed as a coded re-enactment of the Civil Rights Act.[31]

Typically, there is misdirection here. It is true that there is different wording: as we have seen, "not subject to a foreign power" became "subject to the jurisdiction." It can hardly be said, however, that the Citizenship Clause came from a "different political situation," since the goal of securing the substance of the Civil Rights Act in a constitutional amendment was admitted on all sides. Epps recognizes that the Civil Rights Act was passed over President Andrew Johnson's veto; a two-thirds majority of both houses had approved of the bill, indicating Congress' overwhelming support. Since the congressional debates over the Civil Rights Act and the Fourteenth Amendment occurred virtually simultaneously, it can hardly be said that they issued from "different political situation[s]." The political climate was the same for both.

The procedures for enacting the amendment were, of course, different; constitutional requirements for passing amendments are different from enacting legislation. In any case, those who debated the act and the amendment were virtually the same. The principal sponsors agreed with Senator Jacob Howard (who has a strong claim to being one of the authors of the Citizenship Clause),* when he said that "[t]his amendment which I have offered is simply declaratory of what I regard as the law of the land already." The law of the land at the time he introduced the Citizenship Clause was the Civil Rights Act of 1866, which denied birthright citizenship to children born to parents who were "subjects of foreign powers." The debate that immediately followed, as we have already discussed, demonstrated that "subject to the jurisdiction" means "subject to the completed jurisdiction" or "owing complete allegiance" to the United States or, if you will, not subject to a foreign power. The fact that the two acts had "different authors" is wholly irrelevant.

As we have seen, Trumbull, the author of the Civil Rights Act, was a strong supporter of the Citizenship Clause. Epps implies that since he was not the author of the Citizenship Clause his support is less credible, even though he was chairman of the

---

* I had an online debate with Professor Epps in which he insisted that it is well known to constitutional scholars that John Bingham was the author of the first section of the Fourteenth Amendment and that I was mistaken to suggest that Senator Howard had any claim whatsoever to authorship, even co-authorship. As a recognized constitutional scholar himself, Epps should have been aware of a statement that Bingham made in debate on the floor of the House in 1871: "I had the honor to frame ... the first section [of the Fourteenth Amendment] as it now stands, letter for letter and syllable for syllable... save for the introductory clause defining citizens." *Congressional Globe*, 42nd Cong., 1st Sess. (March 31, 1871), Appendix 83 (Rep. Bingham, Ohio).

powerful Judiciary Committee, and worked closely with Senator Howard. Are we to believe that only the author can understand his own legislation? If this were true, legislative deliberation would be impossible. Trumbull had a profound understanding of the Citizenship Clause because he knew, along with its principal supporters – and its author – that it intended to "constitutionalize" the Civil Right Act of 1866. Professor Epps's legislative history, his tergiversations to the contrary notwithstanding, is an obvious attempt at misdirection.

Justice Gray's conclusion in the *Wong Kim Ark* opinion is indeed an anomaly. It contains all of the elements that were debated by the framers of the Citizenship Clause – "subject to the jurisdiction," "allegiance" and "domicile" – that were present in the discussion of the Civil Right Act of 1866. Every serious observer, except for Professor Epps and like-minded ideological scholars, seems to admit that the definition of citizenship in the act was incorporated into the Citizenship Clause of the Fourteenth Amendment.* The only sticking point, of course, is that all of these elements were debated – not in the context of the common law – but, explicitly, in Senator Howard's words, as "natural law and national law."

Besides, if we – as we must – understand "subject to the jurisdiction" as "subject to the complete jurisdiction," meaning "owing allegiance to the U.S.," then Wong Kim Ark, whose parents admittedly owed allegiance to the Emperor of China, would not be a natural born citizen of the U.S. under the Civil Rights Act of 1866 or the Citizenship Clause of the Fourteenth Amendment. The Civil Rights Act, we recall, denied birthright citizenship to children born to parents "subject to any foreign power,"

---

* Senator Trumbull even seems to have had domicile in mind as a limitation of citizenship when he replied to President Andrew Johnson's veto of the 1866 Civil Rights Bill, saying that it would only make citizens of "all persons born of parents domiciled in the United States, except untaxed Indians." See Mark Shawhan, "The Significance of Domicile in Lyman Trumbull's Conception of Citizenship," 119 *Yale Law Journal*, 1352–53 (2010).

which debaters also said meant not owing allegiance to the United States. So, Wong Kim Ark's parents, according to the Civil Rights Act would be "subject to [a] ... foreign power" and thus merely sojourners in the United States. The same status would accrue to them under the Citizenship Clause of the Fourteenth Amendment. Justice Gray's attempt to import the Civil Rights Act and the Fourteenth Amendment into the common law is a fantastic sleight of hand.

## JUDGE HO, ORIGINAL INTENT, AND THE CITIZENSHIP CLAUSE

In 2006, James C. Ho wrote an article called, "Defining 'American': Birthright Citizenship and the Original Understanding of the 14th Amendment."[32] Since his appointment to the Fifth Circuit Court of Appeals in 2018, his article has gained greater attention and authority than it otherwise might have. Judge Ho was nominated by President Trump as an adherent of original intent jurisprudence and the president's confidence in Judge Ho's fidelity to the Constitution seems to have been amply borne out by some of his early opinions. In one concurring opinion, he wrote that "[i]t is hard to imagine a better example of how far we have strayed from the text and original understanding of the Constitution than this case."[33]

"Text and original understanding" are, indeed, the reliable touchstones of constitutional jurisprudence. But Judge Ho did not live up to those standards in his attempt to uncover the meaning of the Citizenship Clause of the Fourteenth Amendment, even as he has recently indicated he understands the high stakes involved. He did write that, "[u]nder our Constitution, the people are not subjects, but citizens."[34] While he provides no acknowledgment, this is a close paraphrase of a statement made by signer of the Declaration and the Constitution and Supreme Court Justice James Wilson quoted in Chapter Two. "Under the

THE CASE AGAINST CITIZENSHIP

Constitution of the United States," he wrote in 1793, "there are citizens, but no subjects."[35]

There is a crucial difference between the two. Justice Wilson was criticizing Blackstone and the common law as providing no legitimate ground for Republican citizenship. Judge Ho, however, argues that the holding in *Wong Kim Ark* was correct – that the Citizenship Clause of the Fourteenth Amendment rests on the English common law, despite the fact that the principal architects of the Citizenship Clause clearly argued that it did not. It would be difficult, then, to argue that Ho was an original intent jurisprude on the issue of citizenship.

Judge Ho rightly notes that the principal purpose of the Fourteenth Amendment was to overturn the *Dred Scott* decision, but he claims, "the amendment was drafted broadly to guarantee citizenship to virtually everyone born in the United States." Indeed, he continues, "[b]irthright citizenship is a constitutional right, no less for the children of undocumented persons than for the descendants of passengers of the Mayflower."[36] He acknowledges that there are two requirements in the Citizenship Clause: born or naturalized *and* subject to the jurisdiction. But, the Judge alleges, this means subject only to the laws and the courts, and nothing more. Since everyone born in the United States is subject to its laws and courts, by Judge Ho's logic, they are automatically subject to the jurisdiction of the United States. His interpretation clearly renders the jurisdiction clause superfluous. If that had been the framers' intention, they simply would have written, "all persons born or naturalized in the United States are citizens of the United States and of the States wherein they reside." As we have already seen, this was exactly the proposal made by Senator Wade on May 23, 1866. But we also recall that the Joint Committee on Reconstruction revised Wade's proposal to add the "subject to the jurisdiction" clause. Judge Ho would have us believe that Senator Wade's original, unamended proposal was passed by the Congress to become the first sentence of the Fourteenth

Amendment. It was not; the Joint Committee evidently placed particular importance on the addition of the jurisdiction clause and intended it to be a substantive improvement on Wade's proposal, not just a superfluous appendage to be ignored.

This is hardly the kind of constitutional construction we would expect from someone of Judge's Ho's legal acumen and someone who professes to be bound by the text of the Constitution and the intention of its framers. Rendering a provision of the Constitution without force and effect is the same kind of judicial activism that adds new rights to the Constitution that are not authorized by the text or a clear inference from the text. Ho has rendered null and void a part of the Constitution that stands in the way of his predisposed views, which – at least in this case – coincides with ideological liberalism. It is not enough merely to consult the latest edition of Black's Law Dictionary under the entry "jurisdiction" to understand the framers' meaning.[37]

Judge Ho refuses to recognize the framers' references to "allegiance" in connection with the jurisdiction clause, criticizing those who,

> claim that the Citizenship Clause protects only the children of persons who owe complete *allegiance* to the U.S. – namely, United States citizens. To support this contention, proponents cite stray references to "allegiance" by Senator Trumbull (a presumed authority in light of his Judiciary Committee chairmanship) and others, as well as the text of the 1866 Civil Rights Act.

Judge Ho helpfully continues: "But the text of the Citizenship Clause requires 'jurisdiction,' not 'allegiance'. Nor did Congress propose that 'all persons born to U.S. *citizens* are citizens of the United States'."[38] There are many misleading and inaccurate statements packed into this short quotation. The characterization of Senator Trumbull as "a presumed authority" because of his position as chairman of the Senate Judiciary Committee and as the author of the Civil Rights Act of 1866 is curious, especially since this was the act, as we have mentioned, that formed the basis for the Citizenship Clause.

Furthermore, it is simply false to say that it reserved birthright citizenship only for the children of U.S. citizens; in fact, it included everyone "not subject to any foreign power" and "Indians not taxed." Trumbull himself used the phrase "subject to our jurisdiction" as meaning "owing allegiance solely to the United States" in the Citizenship Clause debate. We have already discussed at length why Senator Trumbull chose not to use "allegiance" in the Civil Rights Act. It was a deliberate exclusion of a common law term that would have given birthright citizenship to those who owed allegiance to foreign countries – that is, aliens. It is incredible that Judge Ho either does not know this part of the Civil Rights Act debate or does not recognize the significance of Senator Howard's statement that the Citizenship Clause of the Fourteenth Amendment was intended to incorporate the Civil Rights Act.

And to say that allusions to "allegiance" were "stray references" can only come from someone who has made only the most casual perusal of the congressional debates; a detailed reading elicits a multitude of references. All the principal supporters of the Citizenship Clause used the term in reference to "jurisdiction," as our quotations have indicated. While we could cite many more in addition to those we have already cited, we will offer two additional quotations for confirmation. Rep. John M. Broomall, Republican of Pennsylvania, asked this rhetorical question in the Civil Rights Act debate: "What is a citizen but a human being who by reason of his being born within the jurisdiction of a Government owes allegiance to that Government?"[39] The same sentiment was expressed by Rep. Martin Russell Thayer a week earlier, when he stated that, "[a]ccording to my apprehension, every man born in the United States, and not owing allegiance to a foreign Power, is a citizen of the United States."[40]

There is no evidence to support Judge Ho's assertion that only the children of citizens are eligible for birthright citizenship. But there is evidence that children born on U.S. soil to those who owe allegiance to foreign powers or are in the country only temporarily with no intention of establishing domicile are excluded from birthright citizenship. There is no evidence anywhere in the debates to support the tortured conclusion of ideological liberals – and Judge Ho – that the jurisdiction clause applies only to families of ambassadors or foreign ministers.

## DID THE FRAMERS OF THE FOURTEENTH AMENDMENT SUPPORT BIRTHRIGHT CITIZENSHIP?

Judge Ho contends that, "no Senator disputed the *meaning* of the [Fourteenth] amendment with respect to alien children."[41] All agreed, he argues – even those who opposed the amendment – that alien children were entitled to birthright citizenship. We have just demonstrated, however, that this claim is false. Yet Ho believes he has a different proof, this one contained in the debate about whether the children of Gypsies and Chinese were to be accorded birthright citizenship under the Citizenship Clause. The problem here is that he completely misreads this debate. He is uneasy with his conclusion because, as he reports, both those who argued in favor of and against the citizenship of Gypsies and Chinese indulged in "racially charged remarks."[42]

Judge Ho follows closely Justice Gray's one foray into legislative history and succeeds only in following him through the gates of error.[43] Justice Gray had emphasized the importance of construing the language of the amendment itself, arguing against the use of congressional debates to illuminate the meaning of the amendment's language. The reason, I say again, was abundantly clear: none of the principal proponents ever made an argument that the Citizenship Clause was grounded in the common law. Congressional debates would be no help – and, in fact, would be a detriment – in any attempt to support an argument that the language of the Fourteenth Amendment was deliberately founded on the common law. And this was not the only (or even the most egregious) sleight of hand engaged in by the two jurisprudes we are examining.

The question about Chinese and Gypsies immediately followed the debate about whether Indians fell within the jurisdiction of the United States. It was argued, we recall, that Indians owed allegiance to their tribes and, therefore, were not subject to the complete jurisdiction of the United States – and, consequently, not birthright citizens. Even before this crucial debate, but on the same day, Senator Edgar Cowan, Republican of Pennsylvania, was the first to bring up the issue, asking, "[i]s the child of the Chinese immigrant in California a citizen? Is the child of a Gypsy born in Pennsylvania a citizen? If so, what rights have they?" His principal concern seems to have been that Pennsylvania would not be able to restrict the civil or political rights of those who, like the Gypsies, "acknowledge no allegiance, either to the State or to the General Government." In a further query, Cowan asked,

> is it proposed that the people of California are to remain quiescent while they are overrun by a flood of immigration of the Mongol race? Are they to be immigrated out of house and home by Chinese.... [T]hey are in possession of the country of California, and if another people of a different race, of different religion, of different manners, of different traditions, different tastes and sympathies are to come there and have the free right to locate there and settle among them, and if they have an opportunity of pouring in such an immigration as in a short time will double or treble the population California, I ask, are the people of California powerless to protect themselves?[44]

Cowan ultimately voted against the Fourteenth Amendment, whether for the reasons just quoted or for these reasons combined with others is not entirely clear.

Senator John Conness, Republican of California, responded to Cowan's remarks about Chinese immigrants in California.

> The proposition before us ... relates simply ... to the children begotten of Chinese parents in California, and it is proposed to declare that they shall be citizens... I am in favor of doing so.... the children of Mongolian parentage, born in California, is very small indeed, and never promises to be large... The habits of those people, and their religion, appear to demand that they all return to their own country at some time or other, either alive or dead. There are, perhaps in California today about forty thousand Chinese – from forty to forty-five thousand.... Another feature connected with them is, that they do not bring their females to our country but in very small numbers, and rarely ever in connection with families; so that their progeny in California is very small indeed... Indeed, it is only in exceptional cases that they have children in our State...[45]

This was hardly a ringing endorsement of birthright citizenship for the children of Chinese living in California, since the thrust of his argument was that the question was trivial and not worth debating. He admitted that the Chinese living in California did not owe allegiance and formed no attachments to the United States. They did not bring their families with them – not even their females – and they rarely reproduced; it was safe, Senator Conness reasoned, to make them citizens. In fact, it was a matter of some indifference as to whether they became citizens or not. Cowan also had argued that Gypsies owed no allegiance to the United States, and that states should therefore be allowed to discriminate against them in various ways as a matter of self-preservation. For him, it was a matter of states' rights; states should be allowed to deny citizenship and thereby withhold United States citizenship. He appears to have been among a fairly large segment of the thirty-ninth Congress who indulged the implausible hope that the Reconstruction Amendments would not change the Federal relationship.

It is important to note that neither Senator Howard nor Senator Trumbull – nor anyone else – endorsed Senator Conness's view that the Citizenship Clause would include Chinese who admittedly did not owe allegiance to the United States. His speech simply fell flat, carrying no authority whatsoever; it expressed one senator's eccentric view and was apparently not shared by any other member of the Senate. In any case, it can hardly be said to be a strong endorsement – or any real endorsement at all – of Chinese citizenship.

Judge Ho also has recourse to the debates over the Civil Rights Act of 1866 to buttress his claim that the Citizenship Clause extends birthright citizenship to the children of aliens. "In one exchange," Ho relates, "Cowan, in a preview of his later opposition to the Howard text, 'ask[ed] whether [the Act] will not have the effect of naturalizing the children of Chinese and Gypsies born in this country?' Trumbull replied: '"Undoubtedly.... [t]he child of an Asiatic is just as much a citizen as the child of a European'."[46] Here, Judge Ho follows, in much abbreviated form, the account of Justice Gray in *Wong Kim Ark*. Both jurisprudes, however, engage in a careless misreading of the congressional debate and reach a conclusion that is precisely the opposite of the actual debate.

We recall that Senator Trumbull's first version of the act was that, "All persons born in the United States, and not subject any foreign Power, are hereby declared to be citizens of the United States, without distinction of color." An immediate objection was raised by Senator James Guthrie, Democrat of Kentucky, that this definition would naturalize Indians. Trumbull answered that "[t]he intention is not to embrace them. If the Senator from Kentucky thinks the language would embrace them, I should have no objection to changing it so as to exclude the Indians. It is not intended to include them."[47] The seemingly ubiquitous Senator

Cowan was quick to add, "I will ask whether it will not have the effect of naturalizing the children of Chinese and Gypsies born in this country?" Trumbull answered "Undoubtedly."[48]

It is impossible to read Trumbull's remark, in the manner of Justice Gray and Judge Ho, as an endorsement of citizenship for Chinese and Gypsies. Trumbull's "Undoubtedly" is only an admission that the first draft of the language he has submitted is broad enough, not only to include Indians, but Chinese and Gypsies, as well. He agreed with the objectors to the overbroad language that restrictions were needed, and he proceeded to amend his initial language to exclude "Indians not taxed." Nothing was said about excluding Chinese or Gypsies, but it was the unamended – not the subsequently amended (and final) – language to which his answer "Undoubtedly" referred. "Undoubtedly" simply cannot be read as an endorsement of citizenship for Chinese or Gypsies. The "All persons" language of the first draft would have included Indians, Gypsies, and Chinese, "Undoubtedly." The amended language, while explicitly excluding only "Indians not taxed" from birthright citizenship, by a parity of reason, excludes Chinese and Gypsies as well. Justice Gray's and Judge Ho's misreading of "Undoubtedly" is palpable.

Some language was used by Trumbull, who was showing impatience with Senator Cowan, that implied that children born in the United States of "Asiatic parents" who are not naturalized citizens, were citizens.* But Trumbull says this would be the case under the naturalization laws as they currently existed, i.e., before there was any definition of United States citizenship.

The Civil Rights Act of 1866 was the first-ever definition of citizenship and there was some question as to Congress' author-

---

* Recall Judge Ho's remark: 'Undoubtedly.... [t]he child of an Asiatic is just as much a citizen as the child of a European'. " "Undoubtedly" refers only to the unamended text, the remarks quoted after the ellipses in Judge Ho's quotation have no connection whatsoever with "Undoubtedly." His bowdlerization of the quotation disfigures Trumbull's meaning entirely. He has conflated here two widely separated (and unconnected) remarks of Trumbull.

ity to declare the newly freed slaves to be citizens. In any case, the Civil Rights Act's definition of citizenship did not contain, as did the Fourteenth Amendment, a requirement that those born in the United States must also be "subject to the jurisdiction of" the United States, only that they not be "subjects of a foreign power." In the debate over the Citizenship Clause, no one accepted Senator Conness's argument about Chinese citizenship; it is not even certain that Conness himself did; in fact, he made an elaborate case that they did not owe allegiance to the United States. Judge Ho has not demonstrated from the debates that Gypsies and Chinese were in fact included in the Citizenship Clause. His aim was to show that, if Gypsies and Chinese were included, this was certain proof that *everyone* born within the geographical limits of the United States was automatically subject to its jurisdiction. Judge Ho has certainly not carried the burden of proof – or if he has, he has proven it only by rendering the jurisdiction clause superfluous.

## WILL REPEAL OF THE COMMON LAW OF BIRTHRIGHT CITIZENSHIP BRING BACK DRED SCOTT?

In the late twentieth-century and the early twenty-first century there were sustained legislative efforts in Congress to repeal birthright citizenship. President Trump mentioned one such proposal in 2018 that drove ideological liberals to distraction. All the efforts failed, however, mostly due to the efforts by corporations to import cheap and exploitable labor, and a Democratic Party counting on new voters for their electoral victories. From the Left, the campaign of hysteria surrounding the push to end birthright citizenship was mounted in order to further prepare Americans for the desirability of open borders as a principle.

The idea proposed by some Republicans was to use Congress' section five powers to define who is "subject to the jurisdiction," and thereby exclude children born in the United States to illegal alien parents. The constitutional arguments have been rehearsed above. Judge Ho, however, wrote of the grave danger of repealing birthright citizenship for the children of illegal aliens. He wrote in his 2006 article that, if birthright citizenship for illegal aliens is repealed, "Dred Scott II could be coming soon to a federal court near you."[49]

The claim was that *Dred Scott* had repealed the "longstanding English common law doctrine of *jus soli*, or citizenship by place of birth." Repealing the common law of *jus soli* is precisely what Judge Ho thought the congressional attempts to repeal birthright citizenship would accomplish. The thirty-ninth congress had approved the Citizenship Clause of the Fourteenth Amendment in 1866, he writes, "to overrule *Dred Scott* and elevate *jus soli* to the status of constitutional law."[50] Judge Ho's error here is his assertion that the English common law of *jus soli* was repealed by *Dred Scott*. It wasn't. As we have already argued, it was repealed by the Declaration of Independence when it dissolved the perpetual allegiance due from subjects to the British Crown. That was the end of the common law of *jus soli*. Judge Ho should know that, but he fails to see the importance of the Declaration of Independence. Chief Justice Taney realized that the question of citizenship had to be resolved by an interpretation of the principles of the Declaration, but Taney's mistake was, as we have argued, following Lincoln, not understanding the true intentions of the framers of that document which served as the foundation for American citizenship.

Taney did understand, however, that the common law of *jus soli* was not any part of the social compact understanding of citizenship which required the consent of the governed. His mistake was to assume that it was contrary to the intent of the framers of the Declaration that blacks of African descent were not included in the principle that "all men are created equal" and therefore could never be any part of the social compact. Contrary to what Judge Ho alleges, repealing *just soli* would not necessitate *Dred Scott II*; rather it would bring back a renewed understanding of the Founders' understanding that American citizenship was never grounded in the common law, nor was *jus soli* the principle adopted by the Fourteenth Amendment.

## JUSTICE GRAY'S AUTHORITIES AND ELK V. WILKINS (*1884*)

Justice Gray assembles an impressive list of American authorities to buttress his conclusion that the Citizenship Clause is an expression of the common law. Some of his references, however, are outrageous distortions and others are deceptions by omissions. An example of the latter sort is the very first authority cited on the proposition that the Constitution, "must be interpreted in the light of the common law." Justice Gray cites Chief Justice Waite's opinion for the Court in *Minor v. Happersett* (1875), remarking that,

> Chief Justice Waite, when construing, in behalf of the court, the very provision of the 14th Amendment now in question, said: 'The Constitution does not, in words, say who shall be natural born citizens. Resort must be had elsewhere to ascertain that.' And he proceeded to resort to the common law as an aid in the construction of the provision.

Justice Gray, however, should have continued the quotation – since Chief Justice Waite expressed doubt about the clarity of the common law. "At the common law," he continued,

> it was never doubted that all children born in a country of parents who were its citizens became themselves, upon their birth citizens also. These were natives, or natural-born citizens, as distinguished from aliens or foreigners. Some authorities go further and include as citizens children born within the jurisdiction without reference to

the citizenship of their parents. As to this class there have been doubts, but never as to the first. For the purposes of this case it is not necessary to solve these doubts.[51]

So, common law authorities dispute whether the children of aliens or foreigners, like Wong Kim Ark, are natural born citizens under the common law. It is little wonder that Gray choose to abbreviate the quotation.

Hoping to recruit the authority of Chief Justice John Marshall to his cause, Justice Gray cites the case of *The Charming Betsy* (1804) as having, "assumed ... that all persons born in the United States were citizens of the States."[52] Justice Gray "assumed" that Chief Justice Marshall held that position, but it is nowhere stated in the opinion.

Jared Shattuck was born in Connecticut and was taken as a child to St. Thomas, which was then a colony of Denmark, where he took an oath of allegiance to Denmark. He later purchased an American ship, reregisted it as Danish, and renamed it "The Charming Betsy." He sailed for the French colony of Guadeloupe and was seized by an American naval vessel for violating a U.S. embargo on trading with France.[53]

In deciding the case, the Chief Justice said,

[w]hether a person born within the United States, or becoming a citizen according to the established laws of the country, can devest himself absolutely of the character otherwise than in such manner as may be prescribed by law is a question which it is not necessary at present to decide.[54]

In other words, it was not necessary to decide the question of Shattuck's citizenship to determine the outcome of the case. Shattuck may have expatriated himself by swearing allegiance to Denmark. And, having been born in Connecticut before the Revolution and never having returned, it almost certainly means he continued his allegiance to the British Crown, thus rendering his sworn allegiance to the King of Denmark null and void under the common law.

Marshall, however, found it unnecessary to face these questions. The important point is that Marshall nowhere in the opinion ever "assumes" that, "all persons born in the United States were citizens of the States." That is a simply gratuitous exaggeration on Justice Gray's part.

I do not intend to write about all of Gray's citations, although I have examined them and have found many errors of omission and rhetorical exaggerations that imply the presence of the common law where there is no credible evidence of any such presence. Two of the principal authorities that Gray used to support his contention that the common law is the basis for American citizenship have already been examined *in extenso* – *Inglis v. Sailors' Snug Harbor* and *Lynch v. Clarke* – a contention we have argued throughout has no support.[55]

Perhaps most puzzling is Justice Gray's discussion in *Wong Kim Ark* of *Elk v. Wilkins* (1884), which he described as, "[t]he only adjudication that has been made by this court upon the meaning of the clause 'and subject to the jurisdiction thereof,' in the leading provision of the Fourteenth Amendment ... "[56] Justice Gray never deigns to mention that he was the author of the majority opinion in *Elk*, perhaps because the opinion does not argue that the Citizenship Clause of the Fourteenth Amendment owes its existence to the common law. Rather, his argument in *Elk* is derived from social compact.

John Elk was born into the Winnebago Indian tribe, a tribe that was recognized by the United States. He had renounced his allegiance to the tribe and had taken up residence in Nebraska, where he was never naturalized, taxed, "or in any way recognized or treated as a citizen" of the United States or of Nebraska. According to the Court, Elk alleged that he had "completely surrendered himself to the jurisdiction of the United States" and therefore was a citizen of the United States.[57] As the Court noted, however, Elk offered no proof that the United States had accepted or recognized his surrender of tribal allegiance. The Court was insistent that the ascription of citizenship could not be a unilateral or self-selected act: "The alien and dependent condition of the members of the Indian Tribes," the Court concluded, "could not be put off at their own will, without the action or assent of the United States" signified either by treaty or legislation. Neither "the Indian Tribes" nor "individual members of those Tribes" – no more than "other foreigners" – can "become citizens of their own will." Native persons and immigrants "from any foreign State" must first proffer "a formal renunciation" of all former allegiance and then await, "an acceptance by the United States of that renunciation through such form of naturalization as may be required by law."[58]

"The evident meaning" of "subject to the jurisdiction" in the Citizenship Clause, the Court explains, "is, not merely subject in some respect or degree to the jurisdiction of the United States, but completely subject to their political jurisdiction and owing them direct and immediate allegiance."

"Indians," the Court concluded, are "born within the territorial limits of the United States," but are "members of and owing immediate allegiance to one of the Indian Tribes ..." Justice Gray here is paraphrasing the language of Senator Trumbull in the congressional debate over the Citizenship Clause on May 30, 1866, a view that we have seen was supported by the principal proponents of the clause. Justice Gray also cited the Civil Rights Act of 1866, arguing that the children born owing allegiance to Indian tribes were no more eligible for birthright citizenship than those children who are born to parents who are "subject to any foreign power."

Justice Gray certainly knew that the author of that language in the Civil Rights Act was Lyman Trumbull, who, as we have discussed, understood it to mean owing allegiance to any foreign power. Elk cannot declare himself *sua sponte* subject to the complete jurisdiction of the United States – and therefore divest himself of his allegiance to his tribe – and acquire a new allegiance by pledging to the United States. If Elk is deemed to meet the qualifications for citizenship, birth or naturalization and "subject to the jurisdiction," then the United States must first make an offer on the part of the American people; if Elk accepts the offer and gives his consent, he then becomes a part of the social compact and acquires the privileges, the immunities, and the obligations of citizenship. This is the basis of American citizenship, not the involuntary imposition of birthright subjectship, which was expelled from American shores by the Declaration of Independence and confirmed by the Citizenship Clause of the Fourteenth Amendment and its companion legislation, the Expatriation Act of 1868.

Thus in 1884 Justice Gray did not understand the language of the Fourteenth Amendment's Citizenship Clause in terms of the common law. Rather, Justice Gray and the Court (including the dissent) understood the Citizenship Clause in terms of social compact.

In the Court's understanding, consent must be reciprocal. No one can be made a citizen against his will (as in the case of birthright subjectship) nor can anyone become a citizen without the consent of those who already constitute the body politic. This illustrates the constitutional principle that is inherent in the idea of sovereignty, "that no one can become a citizen of a Nation without its consent."[59] We have argued many times that the doctrine of social compact is intrinsic to the argument of the Declaration of Independence, an argument that was more fully explicated by John Adams in the Massachusetts Bill of Rights (1780), which he wrote four years after he and Thomas Jefferson had collaborated in writing the Declaration:

> The end of the institution, maintenance and administration of government, is to secure the existence of the body politic, to protect it, and to furnish the individuals who compose it with the power of enjoying in safety and tranquility their natural rights ... The body politic is formed

by a voluntary association of individuals; it is a social compact by which *the whole people covenants with each citizen and each citizen with the whole people* that all shall be governed by certain laws for the common good (emphasis added).

Justice Gray's majority opinion could almost be read as a commentary on this passage. Needless to say, Adams' account of the compact origins of society and the manner in which citizenship is acquired has no connection whatsoever to the common law. It is difficult to square Justice Gray's majority decision in *Elk* with his majority decision in *Wong Kim Ark*. It is possible that, finding the category of "domestic dependent nations" unknown to the common law, he found that avenue blocked. Still, that doesn't account for the resort to the compact theory of the Founding, unless he actually believed it was the ground of American citizenship at the time he wrote the decision.

Between 1884 and 1898, Justice Gray was involved in three important cases involving Chinese immigration and questions of American sovereignty. He wrote for the majority in two of these cases. All three decisions upheld U.S. laws that restricted Chinese immigration. Discussing the decision in *Chae Chan Ping v. U.S.* which, Gray notes,

was a unanimous judgment of the court, and which had the concurrence of all the justices who had delivered opinions in the cases arising under the acts of 1882 and 1884, it appears to be impossible to hold that a Chinese laborer acquired, under any of treaties or acts of Congress, any right, as a denizen or otherwise, to be and remain in this country, except by license, permission and sufferance of Congress, to be withdrawn whenever, in its opinion, the public welfare might require it.[60]

He then has recourse to the law of nations after his strong paean to national sovereignty:

> By the law of nations, doubtless, aliens residing in a country, with the intention of making it a permanent place of abode, acquire, in one sense, a domicil there; and, while they are permitted by the nation to retain such a residence and domicil, are subject to its laws, and may invoke its protection against other nations. This is recognized by those publicists who ... maintain in the strongest terms the right of the nation to expel any or all aliens at its pleasure [citing *inter alia* 1 Vattel, Law of Nations, ch. 19 § 213].[61]

Vattel, of course, did not support *jus soli*, but Gray was developing the idea of domicile, which, as we have seen, played such an important part the *Wong Kim Ark* decision. The Emperor of China adhered to the system of birthright subjectship and did not allow his subjects to acquire citizenship in other countries. In any case, it is not certain that many Chinese would have sought American citizenship. How Justice Gray came to believe that Americans wanted common law citizenship is still a mystery.

Near the end of his opinion in *Wong Kim Ark*, Justice Gray mentions the Expatriation Act of 1868. After acquiring birthright citizenship in the United States under the common law understanding of the Citizenship Clause, nothing has happened that might have led to the forfeiture of Wong Kim Ark's citizenship. "No doubt," Justice Gray avers,

> he might himself, after coming of age, renounce this citizenship, and become a citizen of the country of his parents, or any other country; for by our law, as solemnly declared by Congress, "the right of expatriation is a natural and inherent right of all people" and any declaration,

instruction, opinion, order, or decision of any officer of
the United Sates which denies, restricts, impairs, or questions the right of expatriation, is declared inconsistent
with the fundamental principles of the Republic.[62]

This reference to expatriation poses something of a dilemma for
Justice Gray. He undoubtedly knew that expatriation was utterly
inconsistent with the tenets of the common law – although, as we
saw in Chapter Two – *Lynch v. Clarke* tried to reconcile the two
(though not without some considerable difficulty). Gray here
speaks of expatriation as being part of, "the fundamental principles of the Republic." This was the view of those who debated
the Expatriation Act. However, the architects of the act saw its
purpose as the confirmation that the common law was never a
part of American citizenship. Blackstone was regarded as having
perpetuated a "feudal doctrine" in which expatriation was
impossible without the consent of the king. This doctrine was
determined to be at war with the principles of American constitutionalism and against natural right.

I previously described the Expatriation Act as companion legislation to the Citizenship Clause. If citizenship is based on consent, then it must be possible, as we saw Jefferson argue, to
withdraw consent and exercise the natural right to leave the
country where chance and not choice has placed you. How can
Gray agree that expatriation is a natural right without rejecting
the common law? I say this shows a fundamental misunderstand-
ing on Gray's part.

## CHIEF JUSTICE MELVILLE FULLER DISSENTS

The Chief Justice stated that it was an accepted general principle
that, "[m]anifestly, when the sovereignty of the Crown was
thrown off and an independent government established, every
rule of the common law and every statute of England obtaining

in the colonies, in derogation of the principles on which the new government was founded, was abrogated."[63] This was most obvious in the common law's "permanent tie of allegiance."[64]

The "principles" to which Fuller refers were, of course, the Declaration of Independence's announcement that the American people were absolved of all allegiance to the British Crown. This meant that America had "manifestly" dissolved the permanent tie of allegiance, something that was forbidden by the common law without the permission of the king. Yet, according to Fuller, the majority opinion holds that, "[t]he English common-law rule ... was in force after the Declaration of Independence" and the rule was that, "'every person born with the dominion of the Crown, no matter whether of English or of foreign parents, and, in the latter case, whether the parents were settled or merely temporarily sojourning in the country, was an English subject...'"[65] And, Fuller almost needlessly adds, "[t]he tie which bound the child to the Crown was indissoluble. The nationality of his parents had no bearing on his nationality."[66] Fuller rightly concludes that, "[t]he rule was the outcome of the connection in feudalism between the individual and the soil on which he lived, and the allegiance due was that of liegemen to their liege lord."[67]

"And it is this rule pure and simple," Fuller comments,

> which it is asserted determined citizenship of the United States during the entire period prior to the passage of the act of April 9, 1866, and the ratification of the 14th Amendment, and governed the meaning of the words "citizens of the United States" and "natural-born citizens" used in the Constitution as originally framed and adopted.

But Fuller is adamant that there was no such rule of citizenship that existed between the Declaration of Independence, the Civil Rights Act of 1866, and the ratification of the Fourteenth

Amendment in 1868. The Civil Rights Act, which denies birthright citizenship to children born to parents who are subjects of foreign powers not owing allegiance to the United States, was explicitly said to be the foundation for the Citizenship Clause of the Fourteenth Amendment. Fuller concludes that "if that [Fourteenth] Amendment bears the construction now put upon it, it imposed the English common law rule on this country for the first time ..." Wong Kim Ark, of course, was born in the United States to parents who were subjects of a foreign country and who, by their own admission, owed continued allegiance to the Emperor of China. By treaty "it is the will of their native government and of this government" that Wong Kim Ark's parents "are and must remain aliens." Thus, according to Fuller, Wong Kim Ark's allegiance, having no independent will at birth, would have followed that of his parents. By treaty negotiated with the Emperor of China in 1868, his parents could not become citizens and remained subjects of a foreign government. Under the Civil Rights Act and the Citizenship Clause, Wong Kim Ark himself was not eligible for birthright citizenship.

The Chief Justice asks a pertinent question: "Did the 14th Amendment operate to abridge the treaty-making power, or the power to establish an uniform rule of naturalization?" If, as the majority opinion concludes, the Citizenship Clause of the Fourteenth Amendment is controlled by common law, then that interpretation becomes the supreme law of the land under Article VI of the Constitution, and all treaties and laws to contrary are null and void. The Treaty of 1868 – which disallows the naturalization of Chinese subjects – is then void; similarly, those provisions of the Civil Rights Act and the Citizenship Clause which disallow birthright citizenship to the children of parents who are subjects of foreign nations is also null and void. No one in the congressional debate made the slightest suggestion that the Treaty of 1868 and its various enabling legislation would be superseded by either. No one would have dared to advance such an outlandish proposal any more than he would have advanced the proposal that the Citizenship Clause was grounded in the common law. I believe Chief Justice Fuller's dissenting opinion is indefeasible.

## BIRTHRIGHT AND DUAL CITIZENSHIP

In the 1898 case, *United States v. Wong Ark,* the Supreme Court ruled that the framers of the Fourteenth Amendment intended to adopt the English common law as the basis of American citizenship. The holding in this case was wrong; it was historically inaccurate, contrary to the intentions of the framers of the Fourteenth Amendment, and a clear violation of the principles of the founding of the United States. It should be overruled forthwith.

But even if the opinion in the case cannot be overruled, a reexamination of the majority opinion can be used to support the reestablishment of the nation-state and restore, at least to a limited extent, the distinction between citizens and aliens.

In his majority opinion, Justice Horace Gray was careful to point out that the parents of Wong Kim Ark – who were still subjects of the Emperor of China and by law and treaty could never become citizens of the United States – were nevertheless, "domiciled residents of the United States ... enjoying a permanent domicil and residence at San Francisco." Wong Kim Ark was born in San Francisco and was considered a birthright citizen under the Fourteenth Amendment because he was born within the geographical limits of the United States.

The children born in the United States to parents who are illegal aliens are today considered birthright citizens, although there is no Supreme Court decision directly on point – but there is Supreme Court dicta that may be construed to support such a conclusion. The parents of these children are not "domiciled residents ... enjoying a permanent domicil" and therefore don't fall under the class of persons described in the *Wong Kim Ark* holding – and this holding is still considered to be authoritative. They should not be considered birthright citizens and legislation authorized under section 5 of the Fourteenth Amendment could specify that children born to parents who are illegal aliens are not "subject to the jurisdiction" of the United States, a requirement of birthright citizenship under the Citizenship Clause of the Amendment.

The same reasoning would apply, not only to the children of parents of illegal aliens – who cannot form an intent to remain because they are subject to future deportation and removal that is beyond their control – but to those so-called "birth tourists" who come to the United States with the sole purpose of giving birth and conferring U.S. citizenship on their newborn children with no intent to remain.

It would also apply to those who come to the U.S. on student visas for the limited purpose of obtaining an education, and those who come to the U.S. for pleasure, business, medical treatment, and other purposes with no intention of remaining and who have children in the U.S. All of these restrictions on birthright citizenship could be done by legislation under section 5 of the Fourteenth Amendment, supported by the authority of *Wong Kim Ark.*

An anomalous feature of the United States' citizenship practice is the acceptance of dual citizenship. By law, every naturalized citizen must take an oath to "renounce and abjure absolutely and entirely all allegiance and fidelity to any foreign prince, potentate, state, or sovereignty of whom or which the applicant was before a subject or citizen." The oath clearly implies the renunciation of any prior citizenship or nationality, i.e., the oath clearly does not encompass dual citizenship. But the "renunciation" provisions of the oath have never been enforced. This creates the impossible situation of a newly minted American citizen swearing entire and absolute allegiance to the constitutional democracy of the United States with its guarantee of the free exercise of religion, freedom of speech, due process, and the whole panoply rights guaranteed by the Bill of Rights while simultaneously maintaining allegiance to a regime that is a theocratic tyranny. No genuine citizen can be so conflicted.

No law stipulates that dual citizenship be allowed; it is simply an administrative decision adopted by the State Department. This insult to American sovereignty and independence should be corrected. This could easily be done by law, but prospects for timely action are not good. I advance the idea that it could be corrected by executive order since the State Department is an executive agency and the oath of allegiance is a legal requirement that the executive branch is constitutionally obliged to enforce.

But these would only be interim actions. The real reform is to untether American citizenship from the common law. The framers of the Citizenship Clause of the Fourteenth Amendment said they grounded American citizenship in natural law and national law. By natural law, they meant "the Laws of Nature and Nature's God," the principles adumbrated in the Declaration of Independence. To say nothing of other matters no less important, the common law is not the Law of Nature. In fact, the common law of "subjectship" was explicitly rejected by the Declaration when it reports that the American people are, "absolved from all Allegiance to the British Crown." The common law prescribed "perpetual subjectship" which could never be relinquished. The Declaration of Independence therefore violated the common law of "perpetual subjectship" as Americans became citizens of a new, sovereign, independent, equal nation.

I offer a detailed examination of how the standard view that the United States has always conformed to the common law of citizenship is mistaken, and how that mistaken view came to be codified in the *Wong Kim Ark* case, even though it is abundantly clear that the framers of the Citizenship Clause of the Fourteenth Amendment rejected the common law basis for American citizenship. My intention is to revive the debate about American citizenship so that, even at this late date, it can be restored to its original basis as articulated by the Founders who knew better than today's Progressives the crucial relationship of citizenship to the sovereign nation, constitutionalism, and the equal protection of equal rights, which we designate as the rule of law.

## CHAPTER FOUR

# CITIZENSHIP, IMMIGRATION, AND THE GREAT SOCIETY

THE CIVIL RIGHTS ACT of 1964, the Voting Rights Act of 1965, and the Immigration Act of 1965 formed the core of The Great Society. Together, they became what some have called the "Second Reconstruction." Professor Gabriel Chin, noted that, "[i]n a remarkable fifteen-month span between July 1964 and October 1965 ... these laws unquestionably marked a turning point in American history and dramatically changed American society."

"Of the three," he speculated, the Immigration Act, "may be the least celebrated and the most consequential."[1] Chin is right: the 1965 law has worked almost without notice; but it has had a dramatic impact on the demographic transformation of American society and, consequently, a radical transformation of American politics.

For many years, this demographic and political transformation was viewed as an "unintended consequence" of the act that no one could have foreseen. But scholars have slowly come to the realization that this may have been the "unspoken" imperative of the administrative state. If so, as long-time chronicler of the American political scene Theodore White lamented some years ago, "the Immigration Act of 1965 changed the future of America ... The new act of 1965 was noble, revolutionary – and probably the most thoughtless of the many acts of the Great Society."[2]

In his remarks at the signing of the Immigration Act on October 3, 1965, President Lyndon Johnson said the bill, "repair[s] a very deep and painful flaw in the fabric of American justice. It corrects a cruel and enduring wrong in the conduct of the American Nation." The root of that injustice, the President explained, was "the national origins quota system," a system that "denied entrance ... from southern or eastern Europe or from one of the developing continents."

America, Johnson continued, "flourished because it was fed from so many sources – because it was nourished by so many cultures and traditions and peoples." While the president did not use the same words, his meaning was the same as the mantra we hear every day from progressive politicians: "diversity is our strength."

With the 1965 Immigration Act, our national origins quota system was abolished; the emphasis in the future would be on the areas of the world that had been excluded in the past. After that year, the majority of immigrants would come from the Third World, particularly from Latin and South America and Asia. The demographic impact would be dramatic. As of 2012, non-Hispanic whites made up 63 percent of the population; however, in two of the largest states (California and Texas), they were minorities. By 2043, non-Hispanic whites are projected to be a minority in the United States as well. Can it be plausibly argued that this was part of the unspoken and unacknowledged imperative of the administrative state?

Johnson insisted that,

> [t]his bill that we will sign today is not a revolutionary bill. It does not affect the lives of millions. It will not reshape the structure of our daily lives, or really add importantly to either our wealth or our power. Yet it is still one of the most important acts of this Congress and of the administration.

It is almost shocking to hear this language from a president who always described his own achievements in grandiose terms. How can we understand the way he underplays the importance of the legislation, even as he touts it as "one of the most important acts ... of the administration?" We know, in hindsight, that the "bill" did turn out to be "revolutionary." It did "affect the lives of millions," and we suspect that the president was aware of its future impact. One perceptive commentator, Roger Daniels, noted that it,

> changed the whole course of American immigration history, although it did so along lines that were already apparent for the few who had eyes to see. In addition, it facilitated a great increase in the volume of immigration .... The most striking effect of the new law has been further to increase the share of immigration slots going to Asia and Latin America.[3]

The stated purpose of the Immigration Act, as we have seen, was to "correct a cruel and enduring wrong" in American immigration policies. The unstated purposes of the Act, however, was to change the racial and ethnic mix of the population of the United States – not only as compensation for past racial injustice, but also as a way of consolidating the administrative state by adding to its list of client groups.

Driven by immense pressures of despotism and economic deprivation in their native countries, large numbers of immigrants came to the U.S. from Third World countries, both legally and illegally. These immigrants have a more difficult time adapting to American customs, habits and laws and show less willingness to do so. This means that they are more likely to need the services of the administrative state, which is only too willing to specify the terms and conditions for their adjustment to American society.

In fact, by promoting multiculturalism, the administrative state has encouraged immigrants to resistant to integration into society. Rather than seeking new immigrants' integration within a common American culture, the administrators – and, eventually, the immigrants themselves – demanded that America should change to accommodate those with different cultures. The old goal of the "melting pot" became mocked as a racist legacy in the new universe of multiculturalism. Indeed, demands that immigrants adapt to American habits and manners were derided as "cultural genocide," a product of America's overweening arrogance fueled by the anachronistic notion of American exceptionalism.

The welfare bureaucracy and its allies in the "civil rights community" were eager to perpetuate the dependence of new immigrants, whether legal or illegal. Bilingual education, affirmative action, and other forms of welfare dependency came to the forefront. Hugh Davis Graham remarked that, "[t]he eligibility of 80 percent of immigrants to America for affirmative action programs made a mockery of the historical rationale that minority preferences compensated for past discrimination in America."[4] Furthermore, Graham notes,

> [t]he proliferation since the 1970s of bilingual/bicultural education programs in American schools has further segregated and isolated Mexican (and Hispanic) children from the American mainstream and weakened the acquisition of English literacy and competence in school subjects leading to higher education and advancement in America's high-tech economy.[5]

Most scholars deny, of course, that there was any concerted effort on the part of the administrative state to co-opt newcomers. The policies were piecemeal and the consequences seemingly unintended. But the administrative state has a life of its own; it seeks to extend the reach of its influence and magnify its power, and it does so largely out of sight of the public. Its weapons are administrative regulations and policies of indirection, all backed by the cooperation of a compliant court system. The Immigration Act played an important role. As one administrator explained, without fully realizing it we have left the time when the nonwhite, non-Western part of our population could be expected to assimilate to the dominate majority. In the future, the white Western majority will have to do some assimilation of its own.[6]

The Non-Western part of the American population has already been relieved of its obligation to assimilate; the "white Western majority," however, will soon acquire assimilation responsibilities of its own. These responsibilities will be presented as matters of simple justice – there will be racial and ethnic reparations and, almost certainly, mandatory instruction in Critical Race Theory.

## AMERICANS IN WAITING

In 1982, the Supreme Court handed down its decision in *Plyler v. Doe*, a case involving illegal alien children. In a 5–4 majority, the Court held that, under the Fourteenth Amendment's equal protection clause, the state of Texas may not deny to illegal alien children the same free public education that it provides to United States citizens or legally admitted aliens. To reach this conclusion, Justice Brennan indulged considerable judicial legerdemain in an attempt to abolish the distinction between legal and illegal aliens.[7] He admitted that, like all persons who have entered the United States unlawfully, these children are subject to deportation. But there is no assurance, Brennan noted, that a child subject to deportation will ever be deported. An illegal entrant might be granted federal permission to remain in the country, or even the chance to become a citizen. Considering the discretionary federal power to grant relief from deportation, a state cannot realistically determine that any particular undocumented child will in fact ever be deported until after deportation proceedings have been completed. It would, of course, be difficult for the state to justify a denial of education to a child enjoying what Brennan describes as "an inchoate federal permission to remain."[8]

Thus, according to Justice Brennan's irrefragable logic, once an illegal alien child is brought to the United States and is able to avoid deportation – either by federal discretion, inefficiency, or unwillingness to enforce the law – that child is now entitled to a constitutional guarantee of free public education under the equal protection clause, and his family can insinuate themselves into the fabric of American society and enjoy "an inchoate federal permission to remain." This "federal permission," of course, may have its uncertainties depending upon the ebb and flow of immigration politics, but there will be many immigration advocacy organizations and legal groups who will represent their interests. Illegal aliens in this category are now known as "Americans in waiting,"[9] a designation that began with *Plyler's* amorphous and constitutionally suspect "inchoate permission to remain." The decision was not protested with any particular vigor by establishment Republicans or Democrats of any stripe because it fit the tacit agreement the two parties had on the continued tolerance and even encouragement of illegal immigration.

We remember that President Reagan in 1986 spoke of illegal immigrants, "who must hide in the shadows without access to many of the benefits of a free and open society." However much the metaphor of "hiding in the shadows" has been used to describe the plight of illegal aliens, it has never been as accurate as the advocates for illegal aliens would have us believe.

The "Americans in waiting" have always been "hiding" in plain sight. In 2006, for example, protest marches calculated to bring pressure on Congress to pass a comprehensive immigration reform brought millions of illegal aliens and their supporters out into the public square; they demanded amnesty and the whole panoply of rights usually reserved to citizens and legal residents. "Americans in waiting," it seemed, would wait no more. The demonstrations were designed to be a kind of public recognition that illegal aliens are crucial to the American economy and should be allowed to enter the mainstream of society. They do the necessary work that Americans are unwilling to do, like hard physical labor for low wages and no benefits. Legalizing illegal aliens would, therefore, be a just recognition of the important role they have assumed in the American economy.

The demonstrations were undoubtedly a grave miscalculation. They served only to harden public opinion against comprehensive reform, especially reform involving amnesty and a path to citizenship that President Bush had promised. Bush was forced to retreat from his early promise that amnesty for illegal aliens would be the first step on the path to citizenship.

Unlike President Bush, however, the demonstrators were clear. They wanted amnesty and did not see the necessity of denying the obvious: amnesty was a recognition of their status as "citizens in waiting." What is more fundamental to a sovereign nation than the determination of who can become citizens and who shall remain aliens? Only in the world of postmodern citizenship could illegal immigrants boldly and boisterously take to the streets to demand a law that would challenge the sovereignty of the United States.

This, of course, was a distinction that was effectively collapsed in the *Plyler* decision. The right to determine citizenship and to defend borders is inherent in the idea of sovereignty. Surrender these fundamental attributes and it is a simple fact that no nation can remain sovereign. It is for this reason that the first priority of those who advocate for a universal homogeneous state to attack the idea of exclusive citizenship and the idea of borders.

## IMMIGRATION UNDER REAGAN AND BUSH

President George W. Bush was, in some sense, an advocate for a "borderless world." He often stated that "family values don't stop at the Rio Grande."[10] There are, then, certain "universal values" that transcend a nation's sovereignty. In these statements, Bush's "compassionate conservatism" was on full display; he often said that we should be more compassionate to our less fortunate neighbors to the south. Bush was merely repeating the rhetoric used by President Ronald Reagan when he signed Immigration

Reform and Control Act in 1986. In that signing statement, Reagan remarked that:

> We have consistently supported a legalization program which is both generous to the alien and fair to the countless thousands of people throughout the world who seek legally to come to America. The legalization provisions in the act will go far to improve the lives of a class of individuals who now must hide in the shadows, without access to many of the benefits of a free and open society. Very soon many of these men and women will be able to step into the sunlight and, ultimately, if they choose, they may become Americans.

Two other provisions of that 1986 Act provided for increased border security and strict sanctions against employers who knowingly hired illegal aliens. Although the bill had bipartisan support, only the hopelessly naïve believed that the border control provisions and employer sanctions were serious; neither Republicans nor Democrats were sincere in their efforts to curtail illegal immigration. In fact, the passage of the act occasioned a surge of illegal border crossers hoping to take advantage of further amnesties, no doubt anticipating that amnesties would become a regular feature of American immigration policy.

Reagan emphasized that the Immigration Reform and Control Act was not a deterrent to those who sought to enter legally. In fact, it was a "generous" and "fair" invitation to immigrants "who seek legally to come to America." It was also an invitation to those already in the country illegally to step out of the "shadows" and "into the sunlight"; they would receive amnesty for their violations of America's sovereignty and "ultimately, if they choose," become American citizens.

Thus, the president offered a generous invitation to immigrants from all over the world to come to the United States legally. And, for those who had already come illegally, he offered forgiveness for their trespasses. Reagan undoubtedly calculated that, because it was the nation's decision to give amnesty to illegal border crossers, there was no threat or challenge to United States sovereignty. He often intoned that this amnesty was a "one-time-only" deal. However, he must have known, as many observers at the time did, that a one-time amnesty is not easily contained. It is difficult to argue that an exception to principle sets no precedent, especially when the same set of circumstances will undoubtedly be present sometime in the future. Why shouldn't similarly situated illegal immigrants in the future be accorded the same generosity and forgiveness? And, as every thoughtful policymaker knew, there would soon be new demands for amnesty, and these demands would be followed by charges from immigration advocates. Only a lack of generosity and humanity, one could argue, stood behind refusals to create new amnesties. In fact, both demands and charges followed in quick order, and continue to the present day.

Christopher Caldwell recently summed up Reagan's approach to immigration in unflattering terms:

> "Reagan was tasked by voters with undoing those post-1960s changes deemed unsustainable. Mass immigration was one of them, and it stands perhaps as his emblematic failure. Reagan flung open the gates to immigration while stirringly proclaiming a determination to slam them shut. Almost all of Reaganism was like that.[11]

The Reagan administration did not take an active role in the passage of the 1986 Immigration Reform and Control Act, especially its enforcement mechanisms. The president's enthusiasm for amnesty was genuine, but amnesty was supposed to be balanced, or "paid for" in political terms, by strict border enforcement measures. Public opinion evidenced strong opposition to illegal immigration in the years leading up to 1986, and Reagan had made an electoral promise to control the borders. But as Hugh

Davis Graham pointed out, Reagan was always wary of alienating business interests.[12]

Reagan, of course, promised to represent the public interest by restricting illegal immigration, but he allowed his commitment to business and manufacturing interests to outweigh his commitment to the public. The public, after all, has no lobby – except elections, which presidents and Congress find increasingly easy to ignore. David Jacobson points out something obvious, but nonetheless striking. "On the face of it," he asserted, "the physically most powerful country in the world should be able to seal it borders against illegal entry."[13]

Thus, legislation that involved vital issues of national sovereignty was decided exclusively on the basis of interest brokering – with scarcely a nod in the direction of the national interest, or a concern for the impact that amnesty might have on the status of American citizenship. Interest brokering and negotiating is, of course, intrinsic to democratic politics. But issues of sovereignty and citizenship involve national interests of general applicability and the common good; these issues are least amenable to such politics. They are the issues which most requires presidential leadership, and it was here where President Reagan retreated from his national responsibility. The openness and compassion he expressed in his Immigration Reform and Control Act signing statement was later to become the hallmark of the George W. Bush administration's immigration policy.

But any clear-thinking observer can see that compassion is not a sound basis for either foreign policy or immigration policy. Compassion is more likely to lead to contempt than to gratitude in both policy areas. The failure of the 1986 amnesty should be a clear reminder of the useful Machiavellian adage that, in the *realpolitik* world of foreign affairs, it is better to be feared than loved. Fear is more likely to engender respect; love or compassion is more likely to be regarded as a contemptible sign of weakness. Delays in implementing new amnesties have been treated with contempt by immigration activists and proffered as evidence that the American people are "heartless" – the word Jeb Bush, President Bush's older brother, used to describe the American people because they would not support more amnesties for illegal aliens when he was a primary candidate for the Republican nomination in 2016.

In immigration activist quarters, amnesty – and subsequently "citizenship" – is considered a right that attaches to "universal personhood." Jacobson notes that,

> [t]ransnational migration is steadily eroding the traditional basis of nation-state membership, namely citizenship. As rights have come to be predicated on residency, not citizen status, the distinction between "citizen" and "alien" has eroded. The devaluation of citizenship has contributed to the increasing importance of international human rights codes, with its premise of universal "personhood".[14]

However noble and inspiring the sentiments on the Statue of Liberty might seem, they are not part of the Constitution. The Constitution commands that the interests of American citizens take precedence over any demands emanating from the "world community." The advocates of the universal homogeneous state, however, no longer believe that national security or preservation of the nation-state is a rational goal; rather, national security must be subordinate to other, more pressing goals more compatible with political correctness, such as openness and diversity. These goals have supplanted national security as the nation's priority, even if it means that the nation must run some risk. Open borders serve to demonstrate this commitment to openness and diversity.

## CHARACTER, CITIZENSHIP, AND IMMIGRATION

Thomas Jefferson understood the vital element of character in citizenship and the relation of citizenship to the regime. He proposed this "experiment" in the *Notes on the State of Virginia*:

Suppose 20 millions of republican Americans thrown all of a sudden into France, what would be the condition of that kingdom? If it would be more turbulent, less happy, less strong, we may believe that the addition of half a million of foreigners to our present numbers would produce similar effect here.[15]

Indeed, twenty million Americans thrown suddenly into a monarchy would undermine the regime. Bristling at the idea of unquestioned obedience and enforced obsequiousness, Americans possessing the virtues of republicanism and habituated to self-government would make them ill-suited to be citizens of a monarchy. The addition of this cohort would introduce an element of anarchy into the French monarchy that would undoubtedly force it to become a tyranny in order to survive.

"[W]e may believe," Jefferson posits, "that the addition of half a million of foreigners to our present numbers would produce a similar effect here."[16] Jefferson does not specify who the foreigners might be, but he had earlier speculated that most of those seeking refuge in America would be those fleeing absolute monarchies or other forms of despotic governments. As might be expected, refugees from democratic or republican regimes would be rare. One might think that those fleeing absolute monarchy and other despotic regimes would relish their new-found freedoms and easily fall into the habits and manners of free citizens, but Jefferson is adamant that these refugees will not become good republican citizens – or at least not easily and not quickly. Their emigration should therefore not be encouraged. In the first place, he wrote,

[t]hey will bring with them the principles of the governments they leave, imbibed in their early youth; or, if able to throw them off, it will be in exchange for an unbounded licentiousness, passing, as is usual, from one extreme to another. It would be a miracle were they to stop precisely at the point of temperate liberty.[17]

Refugees from despotism do not make good republican citizens because they cannot easily shake these habits of deference and assume the habits of independence. Those who grow up in despotic regimes are habituated to bowing and flattery in the presence of social class superiors. This becomes habitual and not easily discarded. If they do throw off the habits and manners accumulated under despotism, it is more likely in exchange for "unbounded licentiousness" without regard to civility, with a contempt inspired by class hatred rather than rational and moderate liberty. This kind of contempt is characteristic of anarchy rather than republicanism.

The exercise of rational liberty – the genuine pursuit of happiness – is acquired only over the course of many years of being habituated to republican virtue. Education to republican virtue begins almost at birth; it is not easily acquired, even for those who live their entire lives in republican regimes.

To expect the newly arrived easily to exchange the chains of despotism for the robes of republican virtue is unrealistic, if not wholly utopian. It is better, Jefferson muses, to populate republican America from its native stock. But he knows that is unrealistic; the country is too large, its resources too vast and its population too small. But Jefferson was clear that immigrants must be chosen carefully, preferring those who were emigrating from free regimes. He wanted to admit only those who can contribute something valuable to America's interests and comport themselves according to the principles of republican government. There would be no open borders in Jefferson's vision. First choice would go to those who already possess the habits and manners of freedom; next would be "useful artificers." "Spare no expense in obtaining them," Jefferson declaimed. "They will teach us something we do not know."

Throughout American history, the assimilation of immigrants has proceeded apace. I think Jefferson underestimated the capacity of the United States to assimilate a wide variety of peoples.

According to Abraham Lincoln, it was Jefferson's own handiwork – the Declaration of Independence – that made assimilation such a powerful force in America. Speaking of the American Revolution in July 1858, Lincoln said:

> We find a race of men living in that day whom we claim as our fathers and grandfathers; they were iron men ... We hold this annual [ fourth of July] celebration to remind ourselves of all the good done in this process of time of how it was done and who did it, and how we are histori-cally connected with it; and we go from these meetings in better humor with ourselves – we feel more attached the one to the other, and more firmly bound to the country we inhabit ... We have besides these men – descended by blood from our ancestors – among us perhaps half our people who are not descendants at all of these men, they are men who have come from Europe – German, Irish, French and Scandinavian – men that have come from Europe themselves, or whose ancestors have come hither and set-tled here, finding themselves our equals in all things. If they look back through this history to trace their connec-tion with those days by blood, they find they have none, they cannot carry themselves back into that glorious epoch and make themselves feel that they are part of us, but when they look through that old Declaration of Indepen-dence they find that those old men say that 'We hold these truths to be self-evident that all men are created equal,' and then they feel that moral sentiment taught in that day evidences their relation to those men, that is the father of all moral principle in them, and that they have a right to claim it as though they were blood of the blood, and flesh of the men who wrote that Declaration and so they are. That is the electric cord in that Declaration that links the hearts of patriotic and liberty-loving men together.[18]

All immigrants can trace their lineage to the blood of the Founders through "the electric cord" of the Declaration. Self-government, dedication to freedom, and the measured pursuit of happiness all flow from that dedication. Dedication to those republican morals, habits, and manners – the "father of all moral principle" – replaces descent by blood as the title to citizenship and the motive force for assimilation. But, as the authority of those principles has declined in the United States, so has the nation's capacity to assimilate immigrants. Today, the Declaration is denounced as a document of "white supremacy" by ignorant ideologues; Abraham Lincoln, who restored its principles against the sustained attack of the slaveocracy, is denounced as a "racist."

In retrospect, it is easy to see what a mistake the Immigration Act of 1965 was. It put an emphasis on immigration from Third World countries, whose people would have the greatest difficulty assimilating. They were welcomed by administrative state bureaucrats who convinced these new immigrants both that it was wrong for Americans to expect them to assimilate, and wrong for them to aspire toward assimilation.

The country was on its way to multiculturalism without any political or moral principles to serve as an authoritative guide. Assimilation, not multiculturalism, is the strength of a nation; multiculturalism dissolves and dissipates a nation's strength. A nation-state must have a shared, patriotic conception of the common good that transcends their immediate interests. As Lincoln's speech indicated, that was the Declaration – the principle that "all men are created equal." That "the electric cord" binds all citizens, regardless of race, color, ethnicity or national origins.

Once the nation has cut itself loose from that "sheet anchor" of republicanism, it will no longer have any principles to guide it. If in our current hysteria we condemn our Founding principles as irredeemably racist, we will no longer guide ourselves by the central principle of natural right, that "all men are created equal." Without the natural right principles of the founding, the nation has no future but dissolution and anarchy.

## AN IMMIGRATION POLICY BASED ON FOUNDING PRINCIPLES

During his time in the White House, President Trump offered proposals to reform immigration policies to emphasize the interests of American citizens. Trump believed the United States should, to use Jefferson's terms, prefer immigrants who are "useful artificers," bringing useful skills and contribute to the economic life of the country. This would be a repudiation of the legacy of the 1965 Immigration Act, what many have called the "diversity lottery." As the former president mentioned several times, this is the most destructive immigration policy imaginable.

Of course, diversity has no intrinsic value. Immigration policies should serve the interests of the nation-state; they should not be acts of charity to the world. The integrity of the nation-state is intimately tied to the integrity of constitutional government and the fulfillment of its purposes – that is, the safety and happiness of the people. Securing these purposes includes the protection of rights and liberties and privileges and immunities that are integral parts of the pursuit of happiness.

Those invited to become members of the body politic should have something to offer to the common good. They should not only possess the capacity to adopt the habits and manners of republican citizens, but they should have the wherewithal to be independent citizens who will not become prey to the minions of the administrative state. Full acceptance of American principles as specified in the Declaration and the Constitution are a minimum requirement for becoming a member of the American polity.

A useful occupation that contributes to the American economy should be another minimum requirement. Unskilled or low skilled labor only creates an underclass that shuts out Americans from entry level jobs that provide the acquisition of necessary work-discipline and skills for economic advancement.

Immigration driven by compassion is misplaced. American immigration policy must seek skilled workers who can make an immediate contribution and who are needed to fill gaps created by a dynamic economy. Compassion is sometimes necessary in extraordinary situations, but as a general policy, it only exhibits weakness to the world. No one has a right to emigrate to the United States.

The nation-state is the last refuge of freedom and constitutional government. Maintaining both requires not only wise but difficult choices. The world is rapidly lapsing into chaos, where only a few stable constitutional governments hold out prospects for survival. These governments cannot be the last refuge for those fleeing violence, terror, poverty, and the host of other ills that afflict the world. If these governments insist on doing so – and if they insist on erasing effective borders in the pursuit of that goal – they, too, will dissolve into dysfunction.

# | ACKNOWLEDGMENTS |

I wish to express my thanks to Tom Klingenstein, chairman of the board of directors of the Claremont Institute, and Ryan Williams, president of the Claremont Institute, for making the publication of this book possible.

# | NOTES |

## CHAPTER ONE

1 Nishimura Ekiu v. U.S., 142 U.S. 651, 659 (1892) (Gray, J.).

2 U.S. v. Shaughnessy, 338 U.S. 537, 542–543 1950) (Minton, J.).

3 Secretary of State John Kerry, "Commencement Address," Northeastern University, May 6, 2016.

4 See Edward Erler, *Property and the Pursuit of Happiness: Locke, the Declaration of Independence, Madison, and the Challenge of the Administrative State* (Lanham, MD: Rowman & Littlefield, 2019), 72–3.

5 Leo Strauss, *The City and Man* (Chicago: Rand McNally & Co., 1964), 127, and Leo Strauss, *On Tyranny* (New York: Free Press, 1991), 20, 22.

6 George W. Bush, "Speech at National Religious Broadcasters Convention," March 12, 2008.

7 Jeremy A. Rabkin, *Law Without Nations? Why Constitutional Government Requires Sovereign States* (Princeton: Princeton University Press, 2005), 16, 239, 254.

## CHAPTER TWO

1 Linda K. Kerber, "The Meanings of Citizenship," *The Journal of American History*, vol. 84, no. 3 (Dec., 1997), 833, 851.

2 See Edward Erler, *Property and the Pursuit of Happiness: Locke, the Declaration of Independence, Madison and the Challenge of the Administrative State* (Lanham, MD: Rowman & Littlefield, 2019), 5–50.

3 Max Farrand, ed., *Records of the Federal Convention of 1787*, 3 vols. (New Haven: Yale University Press, 1966 [originally published in 1911]), 3:61.

4 Ibid., 2:109. See Thomas H. Lee, "Natural Born Citizen," *American University Law Review*, vol. 67, no. 2 (2018), 340–41.

5 William Blackstone, *Commentaries on the Laws of England*, 4 vols. (Oxford: Clarendon Press, 1765–69; reprint Chicago: University of Chicago Press, 1979), 1: 357–358.

6 Ibid., I.354–55.

7 Chisholm v. Georgia, 2 U.S. (2 Dall.) 419, 456 (1793).

8 Wong Kim Ark, 655 (quoting *Kent's Commentaries* 2:258, note).

9 Alexander Hamilton, James Madison, and John Jay, *The Federalist Papers*, introduction and notes by Charles R. Kesler, Clinton Rossiter, ed. (New York: Signet Classics, 1999), No. 39, 236

10  James H. Kettner, *The Development of American Citizenship, 1608–1870* (Chapel Hill: University of North Carolina Press, 1978), 213.

11  Joseph Story, *Commentaries on the Constitution of the United States*, 2nd ed. (Boston: Charles C. Little and James Brown: 1851), 2: §1806.

12  Abraham Lincoln, "Speech at Springfield, Illinois," June 26, 1857, in Roy Basler, ed. *The Collected Works of Abraham Lincoln*, 8 vols. (New Brunswick, N.J.: Rutgers University Press, 1953), 2: 405–6.

13  *Dred Scott v. Sandford*, at 576 (Curtis, J., dissenting).

14  Ibid., at 574–575.

15  Abraham Lincoln, "Speech at Springfield, Illinois," June 26, 1857, in *The Collected Works of Abraham Lincoln*, 2:406.

16  Ibid. See Stephen A. Douglas, "Remarks of the Hon. Stephen A. Douglas, on Kansas, Utah, and the Dred Scott Decision," Delivered at Springfield, Illinois June 12, 1857 (Chicago: Daily Times Book and Job Office, 1857), 9–10.

17  Dred Scott v. Sandford, at 407.

18  Ibid.

19  Ibid.

20  Letter to Henri Gregoire, February 25, 1809, in *Jefferson: Writings* (New York: Library of America, 1984), 1202.

21  1 Sand. Ch. 538, 641 (NY. Ch. 1844).

22  Ibid., 641–42.

23  Ibid., 644.

24  Ibid., 645.

25  Jackson v. White, 20 Johns. 313, 322 (NY 1820).

26  Dawson's Lessee v. Godfrey, 8 U.S. (4 Cranch.) 321, 323 (1808) (Johnson, J.).

27  Jackson, at 323.

28  Ibid.

29  Ibid.

30  9 Mass. 454, 461 (1813). See footnote 11.

31  Respublica v. Chapman, 1 U.S. 53 (Dall.), 56–58 (Pa. 1781).

32  Ibid., at 58.

33  Lynch v. Martin., at 645.

34  Ibid., at 657.

35  Ibid., at 657–58.

36  Julian P. Boyd et al., eds., *The Papers of Thomas Jefferson* (Princeton, NJ: Princeton University Press, 1950-), 2:477.

37  James Wilson, "Lectures on Law," Robert G. McCloskey ed., *The Works of James Wilson* (Cambridge: Harvard University Press, 1967), I:244–45.

38  Lynch v. Clarke, at 656.

39  Ibid. (emphasis original).

40  See ibid., at 665, and the citation of The State v. Manuel, at 672.

41  Ibid., at 652.

42  Ibid., at 653–53.

43  See Harry V. Jaffa, *Storm Over the Constitution* (Lanham, MD: Lexington Books, 1999), 20 ff.

44  Lynch v. Clarke, at 668.

45  James Kent, *Commentaries on American Law*, 2nd ed. 2 vols. (New York: O. Halsted, 1827), 2:39, 49.

46  James Kent, *Commentaries on American Law*, 2:43.

47  Lynch v. Clarke, at 659. See Blackstone, *Commentaries on the Laws of England*, 1:361.

48  Ibid., at 660.

49  Ibid., at 658.

50  Ibid., at 670 (quoting *Inglis v. The Trustees of the Sailor's Snug Harbor*, 28 U.S. (3 Pet.) 99 (1830).

51  Inglis, at 123 (Thompson, J.).

52  Ibid., at 157–58 (Story, J.).

53  Ibid., at 159–60.

CHAPTER THREE

1  Howell's State Trials 559 (1608). Coke's opinion is reported at 607. For in-depth discussion of *Calvin's Case*, see Edward Erler, "From Subjects to Citizens: The Social Compact Origins of American Citizenship," in Ronald J. Pestritto and Thomas G. West, eds., *The American Founding and Social Compact* (Lanham, MD.: Lexington, 2003), 170–181.

2  Calvin's Case, at 614.

3  William Blackstone, *Commentaries on the Laws of England*, 4 vols. (Oxford: Clarendon Press, 1765–69 [reprint Chicago: University of Chicago Press, 1979), 1:357.

4  United States v. Wong Kim Ark, 169 U.S. 649, 698 (emphasis added) (1898) (Gray, J.).

5  *Congressional Globe*, 39th Cong. 1st Sess., 2768–69 (May 23, 1866) (Sen. Wade, Ohio).

6  Ibid., 2890 (May 30, 1866) (Sen. Howard, Michigan).

7  Wong Kim Ark, at 721 (Fuller, C. J., dissenting).

8  *Congressional Globe*, 39th Cong. 1st Sess. 2459 (May 9, 1866)(Rep. Stevens).

9  *The Federalist*, No. 39; see Edward Erler, *Property and the Pursuit of Happiness: Locke, the Declaration of Independence, Madison, and the Challenge of the Administrative State* (Lanham, MD.: Rowman & Littlefield, 2019), 166–182. Schuyler Colfax, Speaker of the House during the thirty-ninth congress, said that the principles of the Declaration had been "placed immutably and forever" in section 1 of the Fourteenth Amendment.

10  *Congressional Globe*, 39th Cong., 1st Sess. 2890 (May 30, 1866) (Sen. Doolittle).

11  Ibid. (Sen. Howard).

12  Ibid., 2894 (Sen. Trumbull).

13  Ibid., 2895 (Sen. Howard).

14  See also Ibid., 527 (Jan. 31, 1866) (Sen. Trumbull).

15  See Erler, *Property and the Pursuit of Happiness*, 173–74; James H. Kettner, *The Development of American Citizenship*, 1608–1870 (Chapel Hill: University of North Carolina Press, 1978), 342.

16  *Congressional Globe*, 39th Cong. 1st Sess., 572 (Feb 1, 1866) (Sen. Trumbull).

17  Blackstone, *Commentaries on the Laws of England*, 1:358.

18  Wong Kim Ark, at 721 (Fuller, C.J., dissenting). See above footnote 7.

19  *Congressional Globe*, 40th Cong., 2nd Sess., 4211 (July 18, 1868) (Sen. Howard).

20  *A Summary View of the Rights of British America*, Merrill Peterson, ed., *Jefferson: Writings* (New York: Library of America, 1984), 105–106.

21  *Congressional Globe*, 40th Cong., 2nd Sess., 868 (January 30, 1868) (Rep. Woodward).

22  Ibid., 967 (February 1, 1868) (Rep. Bailey).

23  Ibid., 1130–1131 (February 12, 1868) (Rep. Woodbridge).

24  United States v. Wong Kim Ark, 169 U.S. 649, 654 (1898) (Gray, J.).

25  Lynch v. Clarke, 1 Sand. Ch. 538, 663, 664 (1844).

26  Wong Kim Ark, at 653; the emphasis on "permanent domicil and residence" was repeated in the statement of the holding of the case at 705.

27  Ibid., at 693.

28  Justin Lollman, "The Significance of Parental Domicile Under the Citizenship Clause," 101 *Virginia Law Review* 455, 465–66 (2015). See John C. Eastman, "The Significance of 'Domicile' in Wong Kim Ark," 22 *Chapman Law Review* 301 (2019).

29  Lollman, 457.

30  *Congressional Globe*, 39th Cong., 1st Sess., 2893 (May 30, 1866) (Sen. Johnson).

31  Garrett Epps, "The Citizenship Clause: A legislative History," 60 *American University Law Review* 2 (December, 2010), 331, 353.

32  James C. Ho, "Defining 'American': Birthright Citizenship and the Original Understanding of the 14th Amendment," 9 *Green Bag*, 2nd Series, No. 4 (Summer, 2006), 367.

33  Whole Woman's Health v. Smith, 896 F.3d 362, 377 (2018) (Judge Ho, concurring).

34  Zimmerman v. City of Austin Texas, 888 F.3d 163, 170 (2018) (Judge Ho, dissenting from denial for rehearing en banc, joined by Judge Green).

35  Chisholm v. Georgia, 2 U.S. (2 Dall.) 419, 456 (1793).

36  Ho, "Defining 'American': Birthright Citizenship and the Original Under-standing of the 14th Amendment," 368.

37  See Ho, ibid., 367, 368. Another highly regarded legal scholar, Professor John Yoo, Boalt Hall Law School, University of California, Berkeley, makes the rather tendentious argument that if illegal aliens are not considered to be subject to the jurisdiction of the United States, understanding jurisdiction in Judge Ho's sense of not being subject to the laws and courts of the United States, they would be free to violate American laws with impunity. This is the kind of confusion results from attempting to render the jurisdiction clause superfluous. Bear in mind that the second mention of "jurisdiction" in the first section of the Fourteenth Amendment was geographical and covered the territory of the States. It guaranteed protection to "all persons" within the jurisdiction of the states not only the privileges and immunities of citizens of the United States but "lives, liberties, and property" as well. Any "illegal alien" violating state or federal law "with impunity" would face arrest and trial for violating laws which are applicable to "all persons" and which are designed to protect the rights and liberties of persons. The idea that illegal aliens are not subject to the law or the courts because they are not subject to the jurisdiction of the Citizenship Clause is a fantasy of perfervid imaginations. All persons are protected in their lives, liberties and properties by the Fourteenth Amendment and illegal immigrants can claim no exemptions from having to obey the law, because all persons are protected by the law against lawbreakers. The Citizenship Clause adopted as the last provision of section one, as we have discussed above, did not mean subject to the laws or courts, but subject to the complete jurisdiction of the United States, owing allegiance to no other country, and not subject to a foreign country. All of the debates surrounding the Civil Rights Act of 1866 and the Citizenship Clause of the Fourteenth Amendment are conclusive on this point. Both Judge Ho and Professor Yoo claim to be adherents of original intent jurisprudence. But on the question of citizenship both of them either misunderstand or ignore the clear intentions of the founders and the framers of the Fourteenth Amendment. For Professor Yoo, see https://americanmind.org/features/the-case-against-birthright-citizenship/settled-law-birthright-citizenship-and-the-14th-amendment/

38  Ho, "Defining 'American': Birthright Citizenship and the Original Under-standing of the 14th Amendment," 372–373 (emphasis original).

39  *Congressional Globe*, 39th Cong., 1st Sess., 1262 (March 8, 1866) (Rep. Broomall).

40  Ibid., 1152 (March 2, 1866) (Rep. Thayer).

41  Ho, "Defining 'American': Birthright Citizenship and the Original Under-standing of the 14th Amendment," 370 (emphasis original).

42  Ibid., 370, footnote 22.

43 Wong Kim Ark, at 697 ff.

44 *Congressional Globe*, 39th Cong., 1st Sess. 2890–91 (May, 30, 1866) (Sen. Cowan).

45 Ibid., 2891 (May 30, 1866) (Sen. Conness).

46 Ho, "Defining 'American': Birthright Citizenship and the Original Understanding of the 14th Amendment," 373.

47 *Congressional Globe*, 39th Cong., 1st Sess., 498 (January 30, 1866) (Sen. Trumbull).

48 Ibid.

49 James C. Ho, "Defining 'American': Birthright Citizenship and the Original Understanding of the 14th Amendment," 367, 378; Ho, "Citizenship by Birth – Can it be Outlawed?" *Los Angeles Times*, March 10, 2007.

50 Ibid., 369.

51 Minor v. Happersett, 88 U.S. (21 Wall) 162, 167–68 (1875) (Waite, C.J.).

52 Wong Kim Ark, at 658.

53 See William Buchanan, "Wong Kim Ark's Ship Comes to Port," *The Social Contract* (Winter, 2012), 43.

54 Murray v. Schooner Charming Betsy, 6 U.S. (2 Cranch.) 64, 120 (1804) (Marshall, C. J.).

55 For other examples, see John C. Eastman, "The Significance of 'Domicile' in *Wong Kim Ark*," 22 *Chapman Law Review* 301 (2019) and William Buchanan, "Wong Kim Ark's Ship Comes to Port," *The Social Contract* (Winter, 2012).

56 Wong Kim Ark, at 680.

57 Elk v. Wilkins, 112 U.S. 94, 99 (1884) (Gray, J.). Elk's tribe was never named by the Court.

58 Ibid., at 101.

59 Ibid., at 103.

60 Fong Yue Ting v. U.S., 149 U.S. 698, 723–24 (1893) (Gray, J).

61 Ibid., 724.

62 Wong Kim Ark, at 704.

63 Wong Kim Ark, 709 (Fuller, C. J., dissenting.).

64 Ibid., 710.

65 Ibid., at 706 (quoting Cockburn, Nationality, 7.).

66 Ibid.

67 Ibid., at 707.

CHAPTER FOUR

1 Gabriel J. Chin, "Were the Immigration and Nationality Act Amendments of 1965 Antiracist?" in Gabriel J. Chin and Rose Cuison Villazor, eds., *The Immigration and Nationality Act of 1965: Legislating A New America* (New York: Cambridge University Press, 2015), 11.

2   Theodore H. White, *America in Search of Itself* (New York: Warner Books, 1982), 363.

3   Roger Daniels, *Coming to America: A History of Immigration and Ethnicity in American Life*, 2nd ed. (New York: Harper Collins, 2001), 341.

4   Hugh Davis Graham, *Collision Course: The Strange Convergence of Affirmative Action and Immigration Policy in America* (New York: Oxford University Press, 2002), 192, 143.

5   Ibid., 184, 83, 173.

6   Martha Farnsworth Riche, Director of Population Studies, Population Reference Bureau, and later Director of the Bureau of the Census in the Clinton Administration, quoted in *Time Magazine*, November 18, 1993, editorial.

7   Plyler v. Doe, 457 U.S. 202, 211 n. 10. Justice Brennan mistakenly conflates the two references to "jurisdiction" in section one of the Fourteenth Amendment: the first, "subject to the jurisdiction," refers to the federal government, and means, as we have seen "subject to the complete jurisdiction," "owing allegiance" to no other country or not being a subject of a foreign government; the second refers to the geographical territory of the states. The proposition that the "subject to the jurisdiction" language of the fourteenth amendment erases the distinction between lawful and unlawful aliens, cannot be sustained either from the congressional debates or from the majority opinion in U.S. v. Wong Kim Ark (169 U.S. 649 [1898]) as Justice Brennan suggests. Justice Gray's holding in that case was limited to children born to parents "who at the time of his birth ... had a permanent domicile and residence in the United States" (at 652). Thus, Justice Gray clearly distinguished between legal immigrants who had "permanent domicile and residence" and those, such as illegal immigrants who would, under the common law, simply be classified as casual sojourners with no intent to remain and whose "inchoate ... permission to remain" made it impossible to form the requisite intent. Brennan also makes a tendentious reference to a 1912 legal commentary, C. Bouvé, *A Treatise on the Laws Governing the Exclusion and Expulsion of Aliens in the United States* (at 425–427), to support his conclusion that the Fourteenth Amendment abolished the distinction between legal and illegal aliens. But the entry cited by Brennan provides no such support. Rather it describes an alien who initially entered illegally but who established a "residence or domicile" and thereby incurred the benefits and obligations that derived from "temporary allegiance." "This does not mean," Bouvé readily admits, "that an alien may continue in a position of allegiance to the sovereign against the sovereign's will. The state may prevent the existence of the condition, by making it impossible for the alien to acquire a residence within its territorial limits, or ... may withdraw its protection by expelling the foreigner. But as certain as is the fact that any such alien resides within the limits of a given

sovereign state, just so certain is it that the mutual relation of allegiance and protection exists. To deny this would be to deny the fact of sovereignty itself, and the existence of a sovereign right, which, like the inherent right of an independent member of the family of nations to expel or exclude aliens." (427) These aliens had acquired temporary domicile and allegiance – albeit without the permission of the United States – unlike Wong Kim Ark's parents who were permanently domiciled residents with the full knowledge and acquiescence of the United States. It is thus a complete exaggeration to say that Bouvé's commentary erases the distinction between legal and illegal aliens. Brennan's attempt to abolish the category of "illegal aliens" derives no support from Bouvé or from Gray's opinion in Wong Kim Ark. Justice Brennan seems to gloss over the fact that the holding in *Wong Kim Ark* is limited to the children of parents who have established permanent domicile in the United States, something we have previously argued an illegal alien can never do. As for the attempt by many commentators to use Brennan's footnote to support the idea that the Supreme Court has endorsed birthright citizenship for the children of illegal aliens born in the United States, the note provides no support, because the defendants in the case were illegal aliens, born in Mexico. Even the most tortured reading of the note would at best yield only dicta.

8   Ibid., at 226.

9   Hiroshi Motomura, "Who Belongs? Immigration Outside the Law and the Idea of Americans in Waiting," 2 *UC Irvine Law Review*, 359 (Feb. 2012), 360–61.

10  White House Press Conference, Jan 26, 2005.

11  Christopher Caldwell, *The Age of Entitlement: America Since the Sixties* (New York: Simon & Schuster, 2020), 113.

12  Hugh Davis Graham, *Collision Course: The Strange Convergence of Affirmative Action and Immigration Policy in America* (New York: Oxford University Press, 2002), 114.

13  David Jacobson, *Rights Across Borders: Immigration and the Decline of Citizenship* (Baltimore: The Johns Hopkins University Press, 1997), 60–61.

14  Ibid., 8–9.

15  *Notes on the State of Virginia*, in Merrill Peterson, ed., *Jefferson: Writings* (New York: Library of America, 1984), Query VIII, 212. Jefferson wrote the *Notes* in 1781–2 in response to questions submitted to him by the secretary of the French delegation in Philadelphia. Jefferson had a limited number of copies printed for circulation to friends while in France as U.S. Minister, but didn't arrange for its publication until his return to America in 1787.

16  Ibid.

17  Ibid.

18  "Speech at Chicago, Illinois," *The Collected Works of Abraham Lincoln*, Roy Basler, ed. (New Brunswick, N.J.: Rutgers University Press, 1953), 2:499.

# | INDEX |

Adams, John, 97
administrative tyranny, 9
Affirmative Action, 12–13, 109
*Ainsley v. Martin*, 45
allegiance: to British Crown (absolv-
ing of), 92, 101; of children, 78; of
Chinese, 74, 81, 89; citizenship
and (Thayer), 85; double, 56; of
Gypsies (Cowan), 87; indefeasible
(Woodward), 72; oath of, 94, 104
105; perpetual, 25, 31, 45, 56, 72,
92; as product of social compact,
59; renunciation of, 43, 96; social
compact and, 45; tribal (surrender
of), 96; under common law, 56,
58, 69; of Wong Kim Ark, 102
American oligarchy (Trump's campaign against), 1
amnesty ("universal personhood"
and), 116
Arab Spring, 10, 11
Aristotle, 1, 22
Articles of Confederation, 31
autochthony (Plato's myth of), 23

Bailey, Alexander, 72
Bill of Rights: common law terms in,
52
Bingham, John, 69
birthright citizenship: push to end,
91; U.S. Supreme Court decision
on, 74, 78. *See also* citizenship,
case against
birthright subjectship, 25–26, 97
birth tourism, 78, 104
Blackstone, William, 24, 25, 61
Brennan (justice), 110–111
Brexit, 14
Broomall, John M., 85

Bush, George W.: immigration under,
112–116; prediction on liberty,
9–10
Bush, Jeb, 116

Caldwell, Christopher, 114
*Calvin's Case*, 24, 61
*Chae Chan Ping v. U.S.*, 98
*Charming Betsy, The*, 94
Child, Julia, 55
Chin, Gabriel, 106
Chinese (arguments over citizenship
of), 86–91
citizenship (case against), 60–105;
allegiance (renunciation of), 96;
birthright citizenship (*Dred Scott*
and), 70, 91–93; birthright citizenship (efforts to repeal), 91;
birthright citizenship (framers'
support of), 86–91; birthright citizenship (Indians excluded from),
67–68, 96; birthright citizenship
(U.S. Supreme Court decision on),
74, 78; birth tourism, 78, 104;
Citizenship Clause (Fourteenth
Amendment), 61, 82–86; Citizenship Clause (liberal interpretation
of Howard's speech introducing),
65; dual citizenship, 103–105; *Elk
v. Wilkins* (Gray's authorities and),
93–100; Expatriation Act of 1868,
71–73; feudal doctrine, 100; Fourteenth Amendment (Ho's purpose
of), 83; Fuller's dissents, 100–103;
Gypsies and Chinese (arguments
over citizenship of), 86–91; law of
nations (Gray), 99; Law of Nature,
105; nation-state (reestablishment
of), 103; original intent, 82–86;

## A NOTE ON THE TYPE

THE UNITED STATES IN CRISIS *has been set in Fernando Mello's Brabo types, which he first developed during a typographic workshop at the Plantin-Moretus Museum in Antwerp and named in honor of Silvius Brabo, the mythic Roman savior of the ancient port city. As legend has it, Brabo defeated the giant Druon Antigoon, who terrorized the city by extorting taxes on shipping and demanding payment to cross the bridge over the river Scheldt, cutting off the hands of those who refused to pay. Brabo defeated the giant and paid him back in kind, tossing his severed hand into the Scheldt, an act that (so the legend tells us) is commemorated in the the city's name: the Dutch for "hand-throw" is* hand werpen, *hence, Antwerpen.* ◆ *A distinctly modern type, Brabo acknowledges the proportions and crisp drawing of sixteenth-century faces like Garamond and Plantin, making it a fine choice for literary texts.*

DESIGN & COMPOSITION BY CARL W. SCARBROUGH